SIMPLE KABBALAH

SIMPLE

KABBALAH

Kim Zetter

Foreword by Ira Steingroot

CONARI PRESS

First published in 2000 by
Conari Press
Distributed by Red Wheel/Weiser, LLC
York Beach, ME
With offices at:
368 Congress Street
Boston, MA 02210
www.redwheelweiser.com

Cover illustration: *The Tree of Life,* courtesy of the
Judah L. Magnes Museum, Berkeley, CA
Cover and book design: Claudia Smelser

Library of Congress Cataloging-in-Publication Data
Zetter, Kim
    Simple Kabbalah / Kim Zetter.
        p.   cm. — (A simple wisdom book)
    Includes bibliographical references.
    ISBN: 1-57324-170-9
    1. Cabala—History and criticism. I. Title. II. Series.
    BM526 .Z47   1999
    296.1'6—dc21   99-28435
                                                              CIP

Printed in the United States of America on recycled paper.

06 05 04 PC 10 9 8 7 6 5 4 3

For My Parents, with Love and Gratitude

SIMPLE KABBALAH

LIST OF ILLUSTRATIONS

FOREWORD

by Ira Steingroot

About halfway through its two-thousand-year history, the course of Jewish mysticism led to the twelfth-century Provençal school of Isaac the Blind, also named, by paradox, "rich in light." Here it assigned itself the name *kabbalah,* meaning "received tradition." My own path to Kabbalah began in 1964, when I first read the mystical nature poetry of Isaac's contemporary, Francis of Assisi. I wondered if such an experience existed in Jewish tradition. I remembered the little I had been told about Kabbalah in Hebrew school and Sunday school, and I remembered that line from Allen Ginsberg's epic poem, *Howl:*

> . . . who studied Plotinus Poe St. John of the Cross
> telepathy and bop kabbalah because the cosmos
> instinctively vibrated at their feet in Kansas. . . .

Well, the cosmos was vibrating at my feet in Toledo, Ohio, and the Beats' fleeting references to their sources led me to Neoplatonism, Symbolism, mysticism, Western occultism, Charlie Parker, and Gershom Scholem's *Major Trends in Jewish Mysticism*. When my grandfather became aware of my interest, he began bringing me volumes of our synagogue's Soncino edition of the Zohar to read. Later he bought me Judah Ashlag's first translated works from the Research Centre of Kabbalah. I can recall one afternoon when I joined my grandfather, the Rabbi, and a group of aged men, each one older than the next, for a Zohar study session. They looked like the crew in Poe's *Ms. Found in a Bottle*. Unfortunately, the text was in the original Aramaic and the discussion was in Yiddish, so I learned almost nothing. Or did I?

My own study of Kabbalah coincided with my suspension of Jewish practice. Observance meant little to me at that time since it seemed to lack the mystical element. Two events occurred that changed my point of view. Professor Joseph Dan, holder of the Gershom Scholem Chair of Jewish Mysticism at Hebrew University, spent the 1977 academic year at UC Berkeley. I was present for all ten hours of his weekly classes for two semesters. My understanding of the texts of Kabbalah increased exponentially, but I still had no definitive answer about practice. At the same time, my son was born in 1978, and I had to make decisions about rites of passage.

I began to practice Judaism again by observing the *Shabbat* (Sabbath) and holidays and by giving my son a Jewish education and making sure he became *bar mitzvah*. Passover became the most important moment of the year, once I set myself the task of reacquiring the skills my grandparents brought to performing the *seder* (ritual meal). Out of this came the insight that normative Judaism was the same as mystical Judaism. It was the *kavvanot* (mystical intention) that transformed "rite words in rote order," as Joyce puts it, into mystical actions and expressions. We did not have to ransack the world's mystical traditions for esoteric customs or practices. We already had them. We just had to understand the mystical meaning that inhered in them at this moment.

Now, in thirty-five years of studying it, that is not the only thing I have derived from Kabbalah. It has been the grounding for every intellectual study that I have undertaken, whether reading Blake or listening to Louis Armstrong or looking at Duchamp or understanding the symbolism of alchemy. To call these studies "intellectual" is to limit in scope what have become my supreme fictions, those things in which I ultimately believe. Kabbalah's importance goes beyond these, though, to include even everyday jokes and casual table talk. Although such things may seem trivial, once kabbalistic concepts permeate our understanding, they can become our most essential and accurate descriptions of the world and our life in it. It bestows a heightened importance upon even the most inconsequential or mundane parts of life:

> . . . even as the trees that whisper round a temple
> become soon dear as the temple's self . . .
> —John Keats

Just so, the cracking of a walnut might remind us that King Solomon in the *Song of Songs* descended to the garden of nuts. In the Zohar, this leads to a comparison of the skull and brain with the shell and meat of the nut. Soon we are thinking about the first three *sefirot* (divine emanations) and the differences between appearance and reality. Once we have been introduced to kabbalistic modes of thought, can we ever again look at anything in this marvelous world without being reminded of an incredibly interwoven net of correspondences? There is a way to look at life as a vale of tears, a drab, dreary, depressing experience, or, alternatively, as a big, sarcastic joke. We all have these moods at times. Kabbalah is a hermetic way of thought that frees us from the either/or dichotomies of happy/sad, good/bad, Apollo/Dionysius. Here opposites are reconciled, and our passing emotions are put in perspective:

> To me the meanest flower that blows can give
> thoughts that do often lie too deep for tears.
> —William Wordsworth

If this volume you now hold is your introduction to kabbalah, you have an exciting adventure before you. May you receive this tradition with all the power, insight, and surprise that are enfolded within it.

Ira Steingroot
28 Nisan 5759

one

WHAT IS KABBALAH?

THE CODED MESSAGE

What is Kabbalah? Nothing short of an answer to the questions of our universe and the ages. More specifically, Kabbalah is the mystical, esoteric side of Judaism that delves into a deeper understanding of the Hebrew Bible (or Old Testament) beyond its literal interpretation to provide us with information about the soul; the nature of God, Creation, and the spiritual world; and about our individual relationship to God and each other.

Kabbalah has received much attention in recent years, often in conjunction with the highly publicized spiritual journeys of celebrities or in magazine articles about hot topics and trendy movements. But despite the bantering about Kabbalah at cocktail parties and on talk shows, not many people know what it is.

Note on the language in the text: Although it is understood by Kabbalists that God is nongendered, for the sake of brevity and simplicity, I have used He and His to refer to God.

While from its recent popularity it might seem that Kabbalah is a fad, it has actually been around for centuries. The Hebrew word *kabbalah* (pronounced kah-bah-LAH) means, among other things, "that which has been received." It refers specifically to secret teachings about the universe and Creation that Moses received from God on the summit of Mt. Sinai some 3,000 years ago. According to Kabbalists, what God revealed to Moses was not merely the Ten Commandments and the story of Creation (Jewish tradition holds that God dictated the five books of the Old Testament—from Genesis to Deuteronomy—to Moses on Mt. Sinai), but a hidden blueprint for the universe: a kind of map depicting the source and the forces of Creation, as well as an explanation about the relationship among human beings and everything else in the universe, all hidden within the text of the Bible. Thus, Kabbalah is a mystical belief system about the world and God that goes far beyond the traditional theological teachings about the divine being and Creation. And, given that Moses was the person who received this knowledge and passed it on to us, one could say that he was the original Kabbalist.

All the questions that have plagued civilizations for centuries (Who are we? How did we get here? Why are we here?) are detailed in the Bible, according to Kabbalists. The Bible, essentially, is a code of the universe. The bestselling book by Michael Drosnin, *The Bible Code,* which finds prophetic predictions buried within the text of the Bible, is a sensational distortion of the concept, but it touches on the basic Kabbalah belief that the Bible is in fact a coded text containing the keys to the universe.

It is, one could say, the original hitchhiker's guide to the universe, which answers all the mysteries that have baffled scientists, philosophers, and theologians for generations, and also provides a how-to guide for living in the day-to-day world. For anyone who would lament that "life doesn't come with an instruction book," the Kabbalists would say, "Look again." The Bible contains all these secrets, as well as instructions for personal development and growth.

The tasks, then, are to decipher the code and unravel the esoteric message within and, with the understanding gained from this message, to apply it to daily practice. Luckily for us, the early Kabbalists have already accomplished this first task. There are dozens of core texts and teachings, written by Kabbalists between the twelfth and seventeenth centuries, that are the basis for Kabbalah learning today. In these texts, the authors have detailed for us their understanding of the world and the forces of Creation based on their careful reading of the biblical texts.

AN ANCIENT TRADITION

In addition to *kabbalah* referring to the secrets received at Sinai, the word also means "tradition," as in the customs, stories, and teachings that a people passes down through its generations. Therefore, when we use the word *kabbalah,* we mean not only the initial words or teachings that God gave to Moses, but all of the interpretations and practices that arose thereafter and were passed down over the ages from Kabbalah master to disciple in an attempt to decipher and comprehend the original teachings and achieve an understanding of God.

While the tradition of Kabbalah goes back for centuries, it has, for the most part, remained a relatively unknown and mysterious theosophy to outsiders. This has been due partly to the secretive nature of many of the original Kabbalists themselves, and, later on, to some mainstream Jewish leaders who alternately embraced and reviled Kabbalah over the years, regarding it as a slight embarrassment to Judaism—something akin to the Jews for Jesus movement—with all its unsettling talk of other worlds, God forces, and harnessing the powers of Creation.

For many years the study of Kabbalah was restricted to men over the age of forty. In some Jewish communities, other restrictions were added: Only forty-year-olds with rabbinical training could study it, or only forty-year-olds with rabbinical training who were also married. The Kabbalah was considered to be too sacred and important for mere dilettantes, too powerful and mind-boggling for the innocent and unschooled, and potentially too dangerous in the hands of the undeserving. Without the benefit of life experience and maturity, the masters believed, one could find oneself adrift in Kabbalah's mind-expanding concepts.

Kabbalah is not a straightforward system like the Ten Commandments, which tell us succinctly to "Do this" and "Don't do that." It's a convoluted system of interconnecting parts similar to the universe itself. The ideas expressed in it weave and spin around each other, and it's easy to get lost in all the concepts that it encompasses. The structure of Kabbalah has often been compared to that of an onion. On the outside, you have the surface skin—the simple story of Creation, presented in a linear fashion. But as you delve deeper, you discover more and more layers beneath the narrative, until you see that it is actually composed of many complex parts and meanings. The story of the seven days of Creation and the Garden of Eden is the starting point. But from there, Kabbalah takes off to touch on everything in the universe—from vegetarianism to subatomic particles; from love and human relations to the union of God.

An attempt to maneuver through the maze of Kabbalah alone and without proper training, the sages believed, could lead to madness. The dangers of getting lost in Kabbalah can be seen in a famous story from the Talmud about four sages who went out to the Pardes (literally "orchard," but figuratively it refers to Kabbalah and the realm of the divine): One of the sages gazed at the divine and went mad, another one gazed and died, the third one became an apostate, and only one—Rabbi Akiva—emerged the wiser and more experienced; actually, it says, he "departed in peace."

Furthermore, to embark on a spiritual journey, to go in search of the soul without grounding or a guide, could make it hard for one to return and function in the everyday world. Therefore, a family and extensive training in traditional Jewish practice were believed to keep the feet of the Kabbalist on the ground. Groundedness is essential to Kabbalah, because there is no glory in getting lost in oneself, in taking flight in the spiritual world and leaving the physical one behind. Unlike some religious practices,

Kabbalah does not denigrate the physical realm and urge followers to reject the pleasures of this world; rather it teaches that true elevation to the spiritual can only occur in the physical world. Paradise doesn't exist in the hereafter or in a far-off time and place; it exists here and now. Spiritual development occurs when we elevate the physical to the spiritual level by experiencing the presence of God in the world He has given us.

Another important factor in restricting the study of Kabbalah was the belief that the code of the Bible essentially revealed the workings of the forces of nature. Genesis, the Kabbalists believed, provided a recipe for Creation. Theoretically, anyone who studied the words closely could find knowledge of how to create life forms. In the wrong hands, such a recipe could be used for evil purposes, to manipulate the forces of nature or to manipulate other people. Indeed, at least one misguided soul by the name of Shabbetai Zvi, also known as the false messiah, did distort the ideas of Kabbalah in the seventeenth century, and thereafter he and some of his followers contributed to the cloak of distrust that was woven around Kabbalah, which has only recently begun to be thrown off.

WHY STUDY KABBALAH?

At a time when life seems to overwhelm us and we feel little control over the events that mark and direct our lives; when the scope of what we don't know about the world only seems to widen with every new discovery we make; when we conquer one disease, end one war, overcome one natural disaster, only to be faced with others, it is only natural that we would begin to question our most basic principles about existence and wonder why we are here.

In the last thirty years, many people in the West have been turning to the East for answers to these questions. In fact, many of the spiritual concepts and Eastern practices that people have embraced in this quest can be found in Kabbalah. Kabbalah's ancient and esoteric message rings surprisingly true in our universal age of searching and contains many of the beliefs that have been part of our understanding of the universe for years—beliefs about the existence of other levels of consciousness and reality, about the soul and the spiritual world, and about the presence of God in every person. Within the teachings of Kabbalah, we find aspects of Tibetan Buddhism, the *I Ching,* and Tantric yoga; we find teachings that touch on meditation practices, breathing exercises, numerology, astrology, reincarnation and resurrection, the energy system of chakras, and even the Zen art of experiencing the moment and finding awe in the everyday. But Kabbalah's concepts aren't limited to spiritual practices. Kabbalah has had a symbiotic relationship with philosophers such as Pythagoras, Aristotle, Descartes, Spinoza, and Derrida; indeed, as scholars like Gershom Scholem have pointed out, much of the cosmology of Kabbalah has been borrowed from Aristotelian and Neoplatonic principles. Traces of

Kabbalist ideas can also be found in the works of Renaissance and modernist thinkers, artists, writers, and poets, as well as the fathers of psychoanalysis, Sigmund Freud and Carl Jung.

While it is fascinating to examine the crosspollinations that exist between Kabbalah and other systems and to delve into questions about who borrowed from whom, it is not our purpose in this book to decide which system originated which ideas. Many scholarly books have already addressed these questions in detail. Suffice it to say that Kabbalah did not emerge in a vacuum; it was a product of the times in which it arose, and the Kabbalists couldn't help but influence and be influenced by those around them and those who came before them. What these similarities might tell us, though, particularly those that appear in different times and different places, is that there are certain universal and inevitable truths that we all eventually find. If various people from various cultures arrive at similar conclusions independently, Kabbalists feel, this can only tell us that they are on the right track. Kabbalists believe, in fact, that we all have different paths to the same truth; despite subtle variations in the route, ultimately we all arrive at the same destination.

SCIENCE AND KABBALAH

Perhaps it is no coincidence that in this time of shifting theological borders, when Bu-Jews (Buddhist Jews) are growing in number and seeking a more mystical understanding of their existence and relation to the universe, we've arrived at a time in which the beliefs of the Kabbalists are ready for mainstream acceptance. Indeed, Kabbalists have long believed that a time would come when the world would be evolved enough to comprehend their teachings. It seems the signs are here. Faith and reason, in the guise of religion and science, have been at odds since the Age of Enlightenment. For decades, scientists and religious fundamentalists have butted heads over their theories of Creation, taking great care to never let science and religion merge. But we have arrived at a point in history in which the gap between science and religion seems to be narrowing. In the last few years, national news magazines have begun touting headlines such as "Science Finds God," and divinity schools have begun offering courses in "Theology and the Natural Sciences." It seems only obvious, then, that a change regarding our view of the universe and the meaning of life is in the works.

Science teaches us that the world is governed by forces and laws of physics over which we have little control, and we have made great progress in learning how to work with these forces to give us a semblance of control over our world and to make our lives comfortable. But what is the point of all this knowledge if all we do with it is create a better coffee or sport utility vehicle or make potato chips that we can eat without getting fat? Is this the divine plan? Olestra and Nutrasweet? The Sports Channel and Batman?

This is where Kabbalah comes in. Kabbalah teaches that we play an integral role in the universe, that we indeed do have great purpose and have great power to affect change. Everything we do has a consequence in the world and every act we commit in the physical world produces a parallel act in the spiritual one. Indeed, Kabbalists say that everything in the universe is interconnected: the universe is a whole, and we are an important part of that whole. As we evolve, so does the universe. It is an ancient spiritual belief that scientists have only recently begun to discover. A paradigm shift in the scientific world has at last awakened researchers to the idea that everything in the universe is part of a related and necessary whole. Scientific relational theories propose that everything, from the immense planets in the universe down to the small microbes in our bathroom sink, are connected in some way; that everything in the universe is dependent on other things around it for its existence; and that there are millions of sub-"communities" that support one another.

To Kabbalists, the discoveries we are making today are simply examples of science catching up with Kabbalah. Furthermore, science is beginning to acknowledge what spiritual practitioners have known for ages: that all the empirical facts about the world will never satisfy our human need for meaning and purpose in life in the way that simple faith does. Albert Einstein once said, "All who seek the truth in the sciences of nature eventually come to understand that there is a power above that is reflected in the laws of the universe." In the end, all our efforts to uncover the cause and effect of the universe will lead us to one conclusion: that God is the essential cause of all. Some time toward the end of his life, looking back on his entire career and everything that he had studied and discovered, Einstein was apparently asked, if he were just starting out, on what mystery he would now focus his talents and energies. What question would he now pose if he were beginning his explorations all over again? He replied, "Is God friendly?"

ORIGINS OF KABBALAH'S CONCEPTS

As mentioned previously, the beliefs of the Kabbalists are rooted in the words of the Torah. *Torah,* which means "teaching" or "law" in Hebrew, refers to the first five books of the Hebrew Bible (also called the Books of Moses or the Pentateuch), but it can also refer more generally to all the holy writings in the Hebrew Bible, including the books of the prophets—Joshua, Ezekiel, Isaiah—and all the psalms, proverbs, and songs.

While Kabbalists examine all the books of the Bible, the Book of Genesis and the Book of Ezekiel are the primary texts they focus on, the former because they say it depicts in detail a very specific and hierarchical process of Creation through which we can understand the workings of the physical and spiritual worlds, and the latter because it presents an account of the Jewish prophet Ezekiel's "face-to-face" encounter with God, through which Kabbalists have gleaned information about the workings of God and how to attain communion with Him. By examining the words and images expressed in these books and looking for deeper meanings beyond their obvious interpretations, Kabbalists have developed an understanding of how and why the world exists, which they have charted out in a complex map called the Tree of Life.

Kabbalah, thus, is a deeper level of meaning of the Bible. It is often referred to as the "soul" of the Torah, and the relationship between the Torah and Kabbalah is likened to the body and spirit of an individual. When we look at a person, we see the person's external, physical self. But inside the body is the soul, which holds the essence of who the person is. Just as we are composed of an inner and an outer layer—the physical and the spiritual—so, too, is the Torah. The narrative Torah is the outer layer, while Kabbalah is the inner layer. And just as the body of a person clothes the soul and serves as the vehicle to carry the soul through this world, the words of the Bible are the clothing that carry the ideas of Kabbalah into this world—they are the means by which we can comprehend the spiritual realm; they are the tangible tools that give concreteness to ethereal concepts.

Don't mistake the body for the person, Kabbalists say, because it is simply a covering for what lies beneath. As the Zohar puts it, "Woe to the man who regards that outer garb as the Torah itself. . . . They who lack understanding, when they look at the man, are apt not to see more in him than these clothes. . . . So it is with the Torah. . . . People without understanding see only the narrations, the garment; . . . But the truly wise . . . pierce all the way through to the soul, . . . which is the root principle of all."

If we read Genesis literally, it tells us that in a matter of six days, God—for no apparent reason other than perhaps to assuage His boredom—decided to make order out of chaos. First He divided the darkness from light, then He created heaven and earth and all forms of vegetation and animal life in it. Only on the last day of Creation, in the last hours before the sun set on Friday evening—the Sabbath eve—He created, seemingly as an afterthought, a tiny creature to inhabit this world: Adam.

But this is a very simplistic explanation for a hugely significant and complex event. It requires the suspension of disbelief and a disregard for the logical and orderly manner that science tells us exists in the universe. Things don't just happen, we know; the world runs on laws of cause and effect.

Kabbalists read the Book of Genesis in a much different way. Adam and Eve and the six days of Creation are an accurate description of what occurred thousands of years ago, they say, but only on an archetypal level. We have to look beyond the literal surface to see what the words actually suggest; and what they suggest is an amazing and complex construction that seems incomprehensible at first, but gradually reveals a very orderly and beautifully harmonious plan of the world.

To comprehend fully the context for Kabbalah and how the Kabbalists developed their beliefs, it is helpful to know something about its relationship to conventional Judaism because, as mentioned before, Kabbalah masters did not live in a vaccum. They were rabbis and Torah scholars, for the most part, who were well versed in the traditional readings of the Bible and Jewish law, and they had a strong foundation in the literal interpretations before they embarked on the spiritual journeys that led them to the knowledge of Kabbalah.

Conventional Judaism is composed of two parts: a written tradition represented by the Torah, and an oral tradition represented by the Talmud, which contains a collection of commentaries on the Torah as well as an extensive code of Jewish law that was originally passed down orally from generation to generation until it, too, was written down between the second and sixth centuries. Together these two parts compose what is called the "revealed Torah." According to Kabbalists, however, there is a hidden Torah, a hidden teaching about the Bible, which was also passed down to Moses. This is the Kabbalah.

Here's how it works. According to Jewish tradition, which counts time from the beginning of Creation (rather than the birth of Jesus as in Christian tradition), God spoke with Moses in the year 2448. Through careful calculation of certain passages in the Hebrew Bible, twelfth-century Jewish scholars determined that the world was created 5,760 years ago (that's 5,760 years ago from today); therefore, 2,448 years into creation, Moses ascended Mt. Sinai for his appointment with God and came down forty days later with the divine revelations.

These revelations were of two kinds: written and oral. The written revelation consisted of the Ten Commandments—a highlighted or bulleted list of laws that God expected his people to follow—and the Torah, or Hebrew Bible.

The first and most basic principle in Kabbalah, and in traditional Judaism for that matter, is that three months after the exodus from Egypt, God dictated to Moses an account of Creation that included all of the momentous events up to that point—and even many years beyond that—which Moses then wrote down and which later became the first five books of the Bible—Genesis, Exodus, Leviticus, Numbers, and Deuteronomy. It is a given that God is the author of the Bible, and that Moses was his ghostwriter.

During the next forty years, while the Israelites wandered through the desert, Moses made thirteen hand-scribed copies of the Torah on parchment scroll, and distributed one copy each to the twelve "judges" or leaders of the Jewish tribes (the twelve tribes of Israel were composed of all the descendants of the twelve sons of Jacob). The thirteenth copy was kept with the Ten Commandment tablets and stored in the Ark of the Covenant, a specially constructed wooden chest that was later housed in the Jewish Temple built in Jerusalem. Every year in late spring, Jews commemorate the giving of the Torah on the holiday of Shavuot, which falls seven weeks after Passover. The giving and receiving of the Torah is the defining moment in Jewish history, because it was at this point that the Jewish nation agreed to enter into a committed relationship with God.

In addition to the history and teachings that Moses wrote down for the Israelites, there was more that he didn't record in writing, but passed on to the Israelites verbally. This consisted of elaborate instructions and commentaries on the Bible that filled in missing details and gaps to aid the Israelites in understanding what God wanted them to do. As with the written tradition, Moses passed these oral teachings on to the leaders of the twelve tribes, and from them the teachings were passed down from generation to generation to the sages and prophets and rabbis of the communities. For nearly a thousand years, these oral teachings passed from person to person, the breadth of the teachings expanding as each generation added to their understanding, until finally they were collected and written down in the second century C.E. in a piece of legal work known as the Mishnah. This became the basis of Jewish law, which described elaborate codes of behavior for all practical aspects of life, such as eating, praying, marriage and divorce, sexual relations, religious sacrifices, property ownership, and work holidays. Altogether the laws encompassed 613 commandments— 365 "Don't" commandments ("Don't take the Lord's name in vain"), and 248 "Do"s ("Honor thy mother and father")—that a Jew was supposed to follow. Later on, the Mishnah was collected into a larger work, along with centuries of commentary

on it, plus legends and homilies preserved over the ages, into a
piece of literature known as the Talmud.

But there was more. During the time that Moses was on Mt.
Sinai, according to Kabbalists, God also imparted to him esoteric information about the cosmos, such as the nature of the
physical and spiritual worlds. This information, which Moses
shared with only a select few, was in fact written into the text of
the Bible for anyone to read, only it was written in a coded language so that only those who searched for it would find it, only
those who achieved the proper level of spiritual development
and understanding would have the expanded consciousness to
see beyond the words.

It is believed that the information was written in code because the Israelites were not yet ready to receive this information. The Book of Exodus tells us that God initially intended to
appear to all the Israelites at Sinai, but the people were unable
to withstand the strength of God's energy, and so Moses alone
spoke to God. Rather than forcing the message onto the people,
the information was hidden in metaphoric language and was
left for a day when the people would be evolved to such a level
that they would seek and find it on their own.

THE WISDOM OF THE MULTILAYERED TORAH

What do we mean when we say the message was hidden in
metaphoric language? According to Jewish tradition, there are

four layers of meaning to the Torah, four levels on which we can read and interpret the Torah: the literal meaning; the metaphorical meaning; the allegorical; and the secret or esoteric. In Hebrew they are *peshat, remez, drash,* and *sod.* The first letter of each of these four words—*p, r, d, s*—spell the Hebrew word *pardes* (orchard). (Vowels are not spelled out in Hebrew but are understood in the pronunciation of a word.) Therefore, in the earlier parable about the four rabbis entering the orchard, we are talking about their delving into the deeper meanings of the Torah.

While the literal meaning is the usual level on which we interpret the Bible, the other three levels are just as important, because they impart a deeper understanding of the surface reading. Take a simple example that shows two levels of meaning: the Bible's description of the Ark of the Covenant, which contained the Ten Commandments. It was said that the Ark took up no space in the Holy of Holies, the room in the Jewish Temple where the Ark was kept. The size of the room from wall to wall measured ten feet. But even when the Ark was placed in the middle of the room, the measurement of the room from the left wall to the left side of the Ark was five feet, and from the right side of the Ark to the right wall was another five feet. We can read this on a literal level and draw the conclusion that the Temple was a miraculous place and that the Ark was a miraculous object that did not take up any space. Or, we can read it on a metaphoric level and deduce that the passage is actually giving us some information about God. The Israelites believed that God's presence resided in the Ark in the Holy of Holies, so the fact that the Ark didn't take up any space might be a way to tell us that God, the Infinite Being, is not space-limited and therefore cannot be measured in the way that we can measure the distance from one wall to another.

Someone reading the text might say, Well, which is it? What are they trying to tell us? Is it that the place was miraculous, or is it a metaphor for the unknowing, immeasurable nature of God? The Kabbalists say it is both. The one doesn't cancel the other. The Temple *was* a holy, miraculous place, and God's essence *cannot* be measured or defined; in one description, the Bible conveys two pieces of information.

Just as scientists have determined that we use only a small percentage of our brain capacity, Kabbalists believe we have only touched on a very small part of the Bible. It only makes sense, given that the author of the work is all-powerful and all-knowing, that the Torah would contain more levels than the ordinary, literal one. As Rabbi Shimon bar Yochai says in the Zohar, "If a man looks upon the Torah as merely a book presenting narratives and everyday matters, alas for him!" The Torah holds "supernal truths and sublime secrets."

The Torah, in this respect, is no different from any other great work of literature—Dante's *Divine Comedy*, Chaucer's

Canterbury Tales—that contain levels of meaning woven into their linear plots. In fact, in most great literature, the plot is just a device for some larger philosophical or sociological message that the author wishes to convey. Take *Gulliver's Travels*—a fantastic, magical children's fable on one level, it is also a sophisticated political satire on another. One of the best examples I can think of is James Joyce's *Ulysses,* a complex, multilayered novel that invokes centuries of Irish and Jewish history, alludes to countless literary, biblical, and mythological references, and contains sly social commentaries about politics and religion, all artfully woven into the rather mundane, soap-opera plot about one day in the life of a cuckolded Irish Jew. In fact, *Ulysses* might be the perfect Kabbalist novel; while it touches on everything under the sun, it inevitably comes down to the quiet, heroic actions of an ordinary, nonheroic man, a theme, as we'll see later, that permeates Kabbalah thought.

Further to these four levels of reading the Torah, the work also has, according to tradition, "seventy faces," meaning that spread among these four levels are seventy possible interpretations of the text. Think about the complexity of this. Seventy possible interpretations means that every passage, every idea expressed in the Bible has seventy possible meanings to it. In fact, in the fourteenth century a work appeared called *Tikkunei Zohar* ("Amendments of Brilliance") that offered seventy different interpretations to the first words of Genesis alone ("In the beginning"), illustrating how the Bible contained so much more than anyone ever imagined.

How is it that there are seventy interpretations of the Torah? One possible answer is that each person brings to the Torah a unique set of experiences and perspective. Have you ever seen a movie with a friend and had an entirely different response to the film than he or she, or a different idea about what the director was trying to convey? Or how often have you discussed a book with a friend, only to think from your friend's interpretation of the story that she must have read an entirely different novel? When any work is approached from two sets of experiences and two sets of knowledge, interpretations are going to vary. Each reader brings a different sensibility to the text; and as we evolve, so does our understanding of the Torah. This is one reason why we refer to the Bible as "the Living Torah." While the text itself doesn't change with time, our understanding of it changes as we undergo change.

But how did Jewish sages arrive at the number seventy? Perhaps because this is the number of peoples or cultures that were said to populate the world at the time the Torah was given. Add to this the Jewish legend that the Torah was offered to all the peoples of the world at the same time that it was offered to the Jews (but other groups rejected it once they discovered all the laws that they would be expected to follow); God would have had to write it in such a way that it would be comprehensible to all seventy of them. Other sages put the number of faces of the Torah at 600,000, which matches the number of Israelites who were present at the giving of the Torah at Mt. Sinai.

The primary teaching of the Bible and the stories within it touch only on a tiny aspect of what is contained within the text. We ignore or fail to see the messages and signs that the Torah is sending us when we concentrate on the surface meaning alone. The Zohar compares the divine words of the Bible to a lovely and coy virgin, who catches the eye of a prospective lover by slowly revealing her mysteries to him. The imagery is erotic, seductive, and poetic. The "beautiful and stately maiden" is secluded in the secret chamber of a palace. Every day, her prospective lover passes by the gate of the palace hoping to catch a glimpse of her, and one day when she sees him, she "thrusts open a small door in her secret chamber" and "for a moment reveals her face" to him before quickly withdrawing it. From that moment on, the lover is entranced.

So it is with the Torah, the author continues, "which discloses her innermost secrets only to them who love her. . . ." When she first attracts them, he tells us, she speaks to them from behind a veil (her words are at first veiled so that they match the listener's level of understanding, and so that her revelations will come to her lover gradually and in a way that will not frighten him away). After a while, she speaks to him "behind a filmy veil of finer mesh" at the level of riddles, allegories, and stories. When, at last, he has begun to understand, the veils are dropped and she stands before him "face to face" and speaks to him about "all of her secret mysteries, and all the secret ways which have been hidden in her heart from immemorial time." Once her secrets are revealed, the lover looks back at her first words and sees the clues that were there from the start, but which he was unable to see clearly then. Everything she did led him to her; every secret was there for him to see from the beginning.

Thus, we come to understand that nothing in the Torah is perfunctory or happenstance. Nothing is there by whim or fancy. "Not one thing may be added to the words of the Torah, nor taken from them, not a sign and not a letter." Kabbalists believe that there are no contradictions or mistakes in the Torah. If there appear to be some, it is not the fault of the Bible, but a fault of our inability to interpret it correctly. If anything seems amiss, it's because we don't yet possess the understanding to read it as God intended. What we don't see in the words today, we will find tomorrow. "Hence," the Zohar concludes, "should men pursue the Torah with all their might, so as to come to be her lovers. . . ."

Why all the subterfuge? Why couch the message in coded language? Why doesn't the Torah just say what it has to say and be done with it?

Kabbalists believe the Bible was given in the way that it was, forcing us to decipher everything in it and delve deeper and deeper to unravel its mysteries, because this is the nature of true learning. We learn best when we are ready to learn, when we seek out the lesson rather than when it is thrust upon us. Kabbalah requires complete presence and commitment of mind to arrive at its deeper messages.

In addition, the Torah was written on so many levels in order to speak to all people simultaneously. One of the foremost teachings of King Solomon espoused by Kabbalists is that you "teach the child according to his way." In other words, every person receives knowledge in a different way, and therefore needs to be taught in a way that matches that method of receiving. When we are allowed to learn in our own way, the learning is more likely to resonate within us, to speak to us. And when something speaks to us in a personal way, we hold onto it. In the same manner, we are meant to approach the Torah through whichever interpretation or path speaks to us, to find in it the words and images that help us comprehend it.

And, lastly, the Torah is complex because the subject about which it speaks is complex. The Torah is a mirror of the message it carries. Its very structure, with all its interconnecting parts and paths, mirrors the structure of all Creation.

It is often asked why, if Moses received the Kabbalah on Mt. Sinai along with the Torah, there wasn't a movement of Kabbalists writing about the Tree of Life and the sefirot around the time of the prophets. The Kabbalists' response is that everything reveals itself in its time. Everything has its season. Kabbalists believe that God reveals only what we are capable of understanding and that He intended that different aspects of the

Torah would be discovered at different times. Not everything was meant to be revealed right away. In fact there's a prayer that Jews recite in the synagogue that says: "May it be the will of God that . . . He shall give us our share in His Torah." Every generation receives its share of the Torah. The Torah reveals itself anew to every generation.

This doesn't mean that what we find in the Torah today wasn't there from the very beginning. The Torah hasn't changed in more than 2,000 years. Simply, our interpretation of it has. Kabbalists say that all the answers we seek are already in the Torah, we just have to find the way to read them.

The purpose of Kabbalah is to teach us that there is a deeper truth to life and to bring us closer to God. The story of Genesis was not given to us to satisfy our curiosity, it was given to us to teach us the path from which we came, and thus to give us a map back to the source. This isn't knowledge for the sake of knowledge; it's knowledge for the sake of enlightenment, for spiritual elevation.

The question is, however, Do we need to fully understand Kabbalah in order to apply its wisdom to our life? The answer is No. Just as you don't need to understand how the mirror in a camera captures images and reproduces them in order to use a camera, you don't need to delve into all the finer, esoteric aspects of Kabbalah in order to apply it to your life. You don't need to decipher the story of Creation or Moses; simply, if you wish to see how the universe works, it is there for the finding.

There's a famous story in the Talmud about a new convert to Judaism who asked the revered sage, Rabbi Hillel, to teach him everything there was to know about the Torah in the time that he could stand on one leg. Rabbi Hillel replied, "Love your neighbor as you would love yourself; all the rest is commentary." This is the essence of Judaism, and it is, at least in part, the essence of Kabbalah.

READING THIS BOOK

There is no prescribed formula for studying Kabbalah. Some people want a firm foundation in the history of the Kabbalah movement in order to understand the background for the ideas. Others begin by studying the texts on the story of Creation, then become curious about the personalities behind Kabbalah and how the Kabbalists arrived at their ideas. Others aren't interested in the history of Kabbalah or the peripheral texts, but simply want to know how to apply Kabbalah to their lives.

Kabbalah encompasses a vast tradition, and it would be presumptuous to suggest that in one book you could learn everything about Kabbalah. You would have to devote a lifetime of studying all day every day in order to touch everything in Kabbalah. This book is intended primarily to give you an introduction to the concepts of Kabbalah and provide a starting point from which you can delve into further practice and study.

The book begins with a historical overview of Kabbalah—where it began and why, and examines briefly the basic literature of Kabbalah, such as the *Sefer Ha Bahir* and *Sefer Ha Zohar,* the two most important Kabbalist works, which give insight into understanding the Bible. In chapter 3 we discuss some of the key concepts of Kabbalah. Chapter 4 provides an example from the Book of Genesis of how the Kabbalists arrived at their interpretations by investigating different interpretations of the biblical text. Chapter 5 discusses the Tree of Life, the main symbol of Kabbalah, which is essentially a map of the Kabbalists' beliefs about how Creation occurred. It is also a map of every aspect—intellectual, spiritual, emotional, physical—of human beings. Finally, in chapter 6, we look at how Kabbalah teaches us about our role in Creation and how we can apply its teachings to our daily lives to gain awareness of ourselves and of the world in general.

As you read this book, there may be things that seem unclear on a first encounter with them. The more you study Kabbalah, the clearer the concepts become. The study of Kabbalah requires a light touch at times. It's like a star that seems to disappear if you stare at it too intently, but comes back into focus if you move your point of vision slightly to the side of it. Kabbalah is like this. Attack it head-on, pursue it too aggressively, and it will frustrate you. But relax and allow it to come to you on its own, and it will reveal itself at its own pace. Kabbalah is not about standing on a mountaintop and meditating on God, or about becoming adept at practicing certain techniques until we have them down—if I follow this recipe and do that, then happiness and fulfillment will follow. It's about living a conscious life, and this is an ongoing, lifelong process.

two

A BRIEF HISTORY OF KABBALAH

IN THE BEGINNING

In the beginning. . . . With these words, the Bible lays out the advent and history of Creation simply and clearly, even poetically. Unfortunately, the beginnings of Kabbalah are not so well defined.

It's not as though the emergence of the modern Kabbalah movement after Moses can be traced to a single year or to a single man who one night had a divine vision and sat down the next morning to write about it in a clear and fully formed manner, the publication of which then attracted a wide following of believers. Indeed, part of what makes Kabbalah so esoteric is the mysterious and mythological nature in which this mystical system emerged, developed, and subsequently disappeared over the ages. The concepts forming the Kabbalah belief system underwent many changes over the centuries before they came to us as the complex system they are today, and their development crisscrossed and meandered throughout history, leaving, at times, only scattered breadcrumbs behind to mark their route.

Tracings of Kabbalistic thought appeared in the first centuries B.C.E. in what is now Israel, then disappeared, only to reemerge in other centuries and other locales as the Jewish people dispersed throughout the world. Kabbalah was alternately embraced and disdained by mainstream Jewish leaders, and was finally left to dwell in the far fringes of the community until very recently, when it experienced renewed interest. While a few personalities stand out as having made specific and significant contributions to the development of Kabbalah, there were many hands involved in its shaping. And the evolution is still not complete.

Kabbalah is constantly being formed and reformed. New minds apply themselves to the ancient texts; new discoveries in science, psychology, and human relationships shed light on old interpretations. This is what makes Kabbalah so interesting: the fact that it reveals itself in new ways constantly; the fact that personal experiences add to the understanding; the fact that we, too, can uncover gems of insight when we stumble upon something in Kabbalah that resonates with us.

Volumes of scholarship have been devoted to theories about exactly where and when the Kabbalah belief system first emerged; yet there are few definitive answers, owing in part to the fact that many of the first Kabbalist writings were authored anonymously and without the existence of peripheral texts, such as diaries or letters, to give us an idea of how the beliefs took shape in the community at the time. Just as Kabbalah itself can drive one to distraction, so can the mere study of its birth and maturation.

To simplify matters, it is generally acknowledged that Kabbalah as a codified movement began in Europe among the Jewish communities of twelfth-century Provence in southern France and thirteenth-century Spain, where the most influential writing of Kabbalah, the *Book of Zohar,* was first published. But the roots of Kabbalah reach back much further. In fact, according to Kabbalah tradition, they go back to the dawn of Creation.

It is here that we have to make a distinction between Kabbalah, the actual body of divine secrets that God passed to Moses on Mt. Sinai and the legends that surround the giving of this knowledge, and Kabbalah the movement or intellectual tradition that developed over centuries thereafter, out of an attempt to decipher and interpret these secrets.

It is helpful to keep these two histories separate, because while the latter is for the most part grounded in documented— and therefore traceable—fact, the former relies much on legend and oral tradition and eludes careful investigation. Regardless of this distinction, however, the two of them together make up what we call Kabbalah.

THE KABBALAH LEGEND

Kabbalah legend tells us that the secrets of Creation and the universe were first given to early man (that is, Adam) at the time of Creation. God made everything known to Adam but then took back or veiled the secrets for several generations after the Fall, because of the copious sinning that characterized the periods of Cain and Abel, the Flood, and the Tower of Babel. In the words of Rabbi Isaac, a Kabbalah sage, "God irradiated the world from end to end with the light, but then it was withdrawn, so to deprive the sinners of the world of its enjoyment."

God then revealed the secrets a second time to Abraham, the first Jewish patriarch, who passed the secrets down to his son, Isaac, and then to Isaac's son Jacob. From Jacob, the tradition passed to his son Joseph. But Joseph, despite his greatness, either didn't have time to write the secrets down or was so distracted by his Technicolor coat that he simply forgot, and the information went with him to his grave. (Some Kabbalists suggest that the coat of many colors that Joseph received from his father and of which his brothers were envious was actually a metaphor for the secret teachings of God that Jacob passed to his favorite son.) For many years thereafter, while the Israelites dwelled in slavery in Egypt, the secrets were withheld and put aside until the people had evolved to such a level that they would understand and be receptive to the teachings. The person chosen to receive the secrets was Moses—the world's first rabbi.

Moses achieved a level of communion with God that was unprecedented since the time of Abraham. His relationship with God was a fractious one, in which Moses questioned and badgered God as much as he obeyed Him. Moses was a man of the

world who experienced the height of power within the house of
Pharoah Seti, as well as the depths of social powerlessness
among the Jewish slaves. It took the experience of both extremes
to give him the balancing qualities of leadership—justice and
compassion—that would bring the Jewish people out of Egypt
and into a new era of self-rule. To this end, God revealed to
Moses the nature of Creation and the spiritual realm, so that he
might pass on to the people knowledge of the source from which
they came, and God also gave Moses the keys to the future, so
that the people might find the path back to the same.

Since it was ordained that Moses would lead the Israelites out
of Egypt but would not step foot in the Promised Land himself,
the Israelites bid him good-bye and crossed into the Land of
Canaan without him. Over the next several generations, they
succeeded, with the help of divine intervention, to win the land
from its unfriendly occupants, and the to unify tribes under a
single monarch (King Saul). The greatest of their military victories was achieved by Saul's successor, King David, who captured
Jerusalem and made it the capital of his kingdom, which
stretched from Damascus to the Red Sea. Around 950 B.C.E.,
David's son, King Solomon, constructed according to God's
specifications the Jewish Temple in Jerusalem (known as the
First Temple), on the site where Abel and Noah had made burnt
offerings to God, where Abraham had brought his son Isaac to
be sacrificed, and where Jacob had dreamt of the ladder that ascended into heaven. The Temple was considered hallowed

ground, and specific rituals governed who could enter and when. Inside the Temple was a special room, known as the Holy of Holies, where the Ten Commandments, which had accompanied the Israelites for centuries throughout their wanderings and battles, were finally housed. The Holy of Holies was the place where God was said to dwell, and where only the High Jewish Priest was allowed to enter, and then only one day a year.

With God secure in his house, and the Jewish people in theirs, a golden era ensued in which the Israelites could finally fulfill God's commandments and realize their potential as a people. During this time, God's presence was readily discernible, and there was ongoing communication between the divine and physical worlds. This was the thousand-year period of prophecy (the years 2448 to 3448 by the Jewish calendar) that had been ordained when Moses spoke with God.

For one full millennium, there was a direct line of communication between the Jewish people and God. Prophets arose in every generation who were selected by God to act as intermediaries between Him and the people. For the most part, these charismatic individuals were members of the upper echelons of society, although a few did come from humbler origins. In times of crisis or important decision making, the prophet would slip into a meditative state of ecstasy and embark on a journey to commune with the divine spirit, who would reveal His will and instructions to these mortal messengers. The journeys, of course, were not physical, but the result of deep meditative trances.

Nothing good lasts forever, however, and after two centuries of self-rule, the Jewish kingdom began to fall into decline. There were constant threatening forces outside it, and growing corruption within it. Over the years, the land was attacked by different rulers, whittling away at the kingdom's size, and as the era of prophecy began to wind to an end, Jerusalem was finally conquered by King Nebuchadnezzar of Babylonia in 597 B.C.E. Thousands of Jews were shipped off to exile in Babylonia, in what is today Iraq; then, in 586 B.C.E., Nebuchadnezzar destroyed the Jewish Temple, but not before Jewish leaders could whisk away for safekeeping the Ark containing the Ten Commandments. (The Ark would never be found again.) Among the exiles sent to Babylonia was one who would become a central figure in Kabbalah, the Prophet Ezekiel.

In the Jerusalem Temple, Ezekiel was a respected priest who distinguished himself in exile as one of the elite who was privy to God's counsel. There isn't much that we know about Ezekiel except that his ability to commingle with God was a blessing for the exiled community; they feared that their estrangement from Jerusalem also meant estrangement from God, who they believed resided in the Temple in Jerusalem and could only be accessed there. But Ezekiel's encounter with God revealed that the people had not lost their connection to Him.

As mentioned earlier, the Book of Ezekiel is one of the most important biblical texts for Kabbalists and is unlike anything else we find in the Hebrew Bible. It describes a mind-boggling, surreal journey of *Clockwork Orange* proportions, in which Ezekiel recounts strange and fantastical visions, like the one in the valley of dry bones where skeletons that line the landscape suddenly begin to jiggle and rattle their bones and reconstruct themselves as flesh-and-blood, or the one in which he sees wheels soaring through the sky (what some people have taken to be flying saucers).

Most important to Kabbalists, however, is the first chapter of his book, which they believe paints a portrait of the prophetic experience and reveals the nature of God. In it, Ezekiel describes how "in the thirtieth year, in the fourth month, on the fifth day. . ." the heavens open up to him and reveal an extraordinary sight. A stormy wind comes down from the north, carrying a great cloud with flashing fire inside it. Out of the cloud emerge four figures who resemble men except that each has four faces on his head—the face of a man in front, the face of a lion on the right side, the face of an ox on the left, and an eagle's face on the back—and cloven feet that shine like bronze. Each figure has two pairs of wings, which they use to fly through the sky. They fly in unison with each other and without needing to turn to the direction in which they move, since they already have a face in every direction. Beneath the cloven feet are four wheels, each with a second wheel at a cross angle inside it, enabling the wheel to move forward, backward, right, or left without needing to turn. The wheels move in conjunction with the figures: If the figures fly upward, so do the wheels; if they zoom sideways, the wheels go with them. It is apparent to Ezekiel that the spirit of the four beings resides in the wheels.

The description goes on and on until finally, in the sky above the four figures, Ezekiel spies the figure of God sitting on a chariot or throne of blue lapis. Ezekiel writes, "Such was the appearance of the likeness of the glory of the LORD. And when I saw it, I fell upon my face, and I heard the voice of one speaking."

God tells Ezekiel that He is to deliver a message to the exiles in Babylonia and then gives him a scroll with writing on both sides, filled with prophecies of doom and salvation for the Jewish people, particularly those still back in Jerusalem. For Kabbalists, the prophecies themselves are less interesting than Ezekiel's description of how he came by them. Kabbalists have honed in on this chapter of the Bible because it differs from anything written by other prophets, and anything out of the ordinary in the Bible is granted great significance.

Numerous prophets had channeled the spirit and words of God before, but none had recorded the vision that Ezekiel did, and certainly not in such precise detail. Why? the mystics wondered. Perhaps because the other prophets felt this preamble was unimportant. If I had a face-to-face audience with the president of the United States, I wouldn't tell you about my taxi ride over to the White House (unless there was something significant about the ride), I'd cut to the chase and tell you the details of what the president and I talked about. But here was Ezekiel going into considerable detail about the weather conditions and tourist sights down Pennsylvania Avenue. He must have had a reason, the Kabbalists decided. What they concluded was that buried within this detailed description, Ezekiel was recounting the realms that one passes through before hearing the voice of God.

Why did Ezekiel go beyond previous prophets to provide us with information that no one else had bothered to give? Kabbalists believe Ezekiel was doing us a favor. He knew that the era of prophecy was drawing to an end and that he was the last of a breed. It seems he had the foresight to record his experience so that someone in the future might pick up where he left off.

Ezekiel's revolutionary words set off an entire genre of mystical musings that focused on achieving the vision that Ezekiel had seen and on discerning the mysteries of the heavens. Rather than just accepting God as an unknowable force, people were beginning to fathom God as some knowable being. Other writers, most anonymous, used Ezekiel as a jumping-off point to devise theories on the character of God, the nature of His heavens, and the means for breaking through barriers to the spiritual world. By studying the steps that Ezekiel described, the early mystics concluded, they, too, could attain divine prophecy. This led to another important discovery about Ezekiel's account: The suggestion that God might be found anywhere by anyone who had the skills to reach him. God was accessible through a power that we possessed, if only we could learn how to develop it.

This early era of mysticism, which began sometime around the first century B.C.E., marked the beginnings of spiritual awakening and continued for nearly a millennium into the tenth century C.E. It became known as *Merkavah* mysticism, stemming from the Hebrew word for "chariot" that Ezekiel used to describe the moving throne upon which God sat.

Merkavah mystics were not members of the general masses, but rather were elite, highly educated orthodox rabbis who lived devout lives and conducted their discussions of esotericism in private circles, wary that the information might be passed to the wrong hands or garner criticism from traditional circles who considered such discussions outside the realm of normal Judaism. The writings of Merkavah mystics took many forms— from apocalyptic forewarnings to spiritual hymns—and did not represent an organized movement by any means, but there were enough similarities among the texts—angels and demons, multiple realms of heaven—to suggest a belief system in the infant stages of development. Many of the accounts were spiritual travelogues from explorers who had visited the supernal world and then returned to write about it. They provided instructions for achieving states of ecstasy and described fantastic journeys through seven heavens bathed in divine light. In one, an angel tells the mystical journeyman, "If you rejoice over this light, imagine how much more you will rejoice in the seventh heaven when you see the light of God," suggesting, perhaps, our source for the expression "in seventh heaven." Whatever the experience, the writings make clear that this is knowledge that cannot be obtained through mundane intellectual study. It comes only through deep meditation, through releasing the rational nature and allowing the spiritual nature to soar in the realms of the divine.

We should note, here, that mysticism during this period was not a phenomenon unique to Judaism. A belief in the transcendental experience was common to many people at the time, and Jews and non-Jews alike were attempting to apprehend the nature of the spiritual world. But the difference with Jewish mysticism, as preeminent Kabbalah scholar Gershom Scholem has pointed out, lay in the fact that it remained linked to a particular people and tradition, whereas other mystical movements were not rooted to any one people or tradition.

SEFER YETZIRAH

It is within this Merkavah tradition that a second important development in Kabbalah emerged sometime between the third and sixth centuries C.E., with the circulation of a manuscript called *Sefer Yetzirah* ("Book of Creation"). No one knows who wrote the text, but *Sefer Yetzirah*—a short essay, really, that runs only a few pages long—is the first mystical work we have that lays out a theory of Creation and the order of the universe. It is from this work that later Kabbalism derives much of its vocabulary, including the naming of the sefirot, the ten elemental energy forces that are the characteristics of God and the agents of all Creation.

The author, interpreting the text of Genesis, proposes that Creation occurred on two levels or in two stages: first, at the level of conception (before there can be action there has to be an idea or a concept); then at the level of physical manifestation of that concept. God had an idea, and then He made that idea reality. The process of getting from concept to reality involved the ten sefirot and the Hebrew alphabet, which are the instruments of Creation.

It is a sophisticated theory of Creation based on language, speech, and sounds ("God said, 'Let there be light,' and there was light"). The author speculates that Creation occurred via thirty-two paths; he arrives at the number thirty-two by adding the twenty-two letters of the Hebrew alphabet and the ten sefirot (*sefirot,* pronounced sphi-ROTE, is plural for the Hebrew *sefira* and comes from the verb "to count"). What this means is that through interaction between the letters of the alphabet (which have their own internal force or power) and the powers of God, all Creation came into being. The number thirty-two can also be arrived at by adding the numerical equivalents of the first and last Hebrew letters of the Bible: *bet,* the first letter of Genesis (with a value of 2) and *lamed,* the last letter of Deuteronomy (with a value of 30). The implication is that the secrets of Creation are to be found within and between all the letters of the Bible; the thirty-two paths of wisdom are found in the Torah.

Ultimately, however, *Sefer Yetzirah* isn't just offering an interpretation of Genesis; it is instructing readers in the art of creative magic. Encoded in Genesis, the author suggests, is a recipe for creation that anyone can follow. Learn the process and remix the elements according to a precise formula, and you too could develop godlike powers, though certainly on a lesser level. The book's final chapter offers a summary in which the author asserts that all these secrets were given long ago to Abraham by God and that Abraham was the first practitioner of the Creation magic. (Some people have taken this to suggest that Abraham was actually the author of *Sefer Yetzirah*, but scholars reject this.)

Later on, we will discuss how exactly it is that letters can create. However, it is important to note here that numbers and letters play a significant role in *Yetzirah*. Numbers, of course, have a much wider importance in the theories of the Greek philosopher and mathematician Pythagoras, who lived some 900 years prior to the appearance of *Yetzirah* and who asserted that all of the universe could be reduced to numerical formulas—a theory that has been borne out by modern science, with the development of genetic coding and the atomic numbering system for chemical elements. What this means, simply, is that some of the basic concepts of Kabbalah had their roots in philosophical ideas that were already circulating at the time Kabbalah mysticism was developing.

Yetzirah was not intended for mass consumption, but for elite rabbis who had deep understanding of the written and oral traditions. While some in the community feared that the book promoted the conjuring of black magic, the work was taken very seriously and paved the way for ideas that would later become the core of Kabbalist Creation theory. Some scholars tend to negate the connection between the majority of early mystical writings and later twelfth-century Kabbalah, but it's hard not to see the influence that the works of Merkavah mysticism had, particularly since many of the ideas espoused in *Sefer Yetzirah* are elemental to later Kabbalist texts. The ideas, perhaps, were still a bit premature at this stage and needed to incubate, but they are definitely discernible as the impetus for concepts that appear later on. There is at least one main difference, however, between early Merkavah mysticism and later Kabbalah, and that is that the former addressed humans, for the most part, only insofar as they played a role in receiving information from God. The inner nature of human beings and their relationship to God did not seem to interest the Merkavah mystics, while Kabbalists of the Middle Ages devoted much energy to this topic.

RABBI AKIVA

Before the Merkavah mystics would begin their musings, however, there were still a number of events that would occur for the Jewish people in exile and in the remnant communities of Judea. Following the defeat of the Babylonians in 539 B.C.E., some forty-seven years after the destruction of the Temple, the conquering Persian ruler allowed the Jewish exiles to return to Judea and rebuild their Temple. This new temple was completed some time around 515 B.C.E. and became known as the Second Temple. For many years thereafter, during Persian rule and under subsequent conquerors after the Persian empire fell, the Israelites lived fairly autonomously. All this changed, however, when the Romans arrived in 63 B.C.E.

Roman policy toward the Jews throughout the first hundred years of its rule went through several stages, beginning rather benevolently but gradually progressing to increased repression. Oppressive and unequal taxation, corrupt local Roman rulers, and the demand for strict loyalty to Rome resulted in escalating clashes between Roman authorities and Jewish subjects, which culminated in an all-out Jewish revolt that engulfed the entire land. Roman legions were sent in to quell the revolt and, in 70 C.E., the Roman general Titus conquered Jerusalem and leveled the Second Temple, sending Jews fleeing to other parts of Judea.

Out of this turmoil emerged another key Kabbalah figure, Rabbi Akiva ben Yoseph, a respected Jewish sage and the foremost scholar of his time, who lived in early Palestine from 40 to 135 C.E. and was head of the Sanhedrin council, the top Jewish legal council. Akiva is best remembered, for our purposes, for his starring role in two Jewish legends. The first regards Moses on Mt. Sinai. When Moses ascended the mountain to receive the Torah from God he found God preoccupied with ornamenting the letters of the Torah with decorative marks that resembled little crowns. Moses asked God, Why the crowns? And God replied that in the future there would live a man who would find great wisdom and significance in these crowns and base numerous laws upon them. When Moses beseeched God to show him this man, God showed him a vision of Rabbi Akiva. The second legend is the one previously mentioned about the four sages who ventured into the Pardes, and only Rabbi Akiva exited in peace.

Akiva was an extremely simple, modest, and devout man who lived most of his life as an uneducated peasant who abhorred scholars. "Had I a scholar in my power," he was known to have said, "I would maul him like an ass." He didn't even know the alphabet until, one day at the age of around thirty or thirty-five, he decided to immerse himself in the Torah to fulfill a promise to his wife Rachel. It is said that he was so humble he sat patiently in a classroom full of small boys, among them his own son, in order to learn how to read and write Hebrew from their teacher. He studied diligently for some twelve years, and also explored esoteric aspects of the Torah, as did many other rabbis of his time. He concluded that since the Torah emanated from God, it could not contain any errors, and that everything in it was intentional. His command of the alphabet eventually led him to make one of the more astounding declarations about the language of the Bible: that encoded in the words and letters themselves, even the shapes of the letters, one could find great meaning.

The fact that Akiva was the leader of the Sanhedrin is evidence that early mystics were far from being zealous heretics or community outsiders; indeed, they were often respected scholars who, out of spiritual devotion, were simply delving into the sacred texts to find deeper meaning in the words of God. Akiva would eventually die by terrible torture around 135 C.E. at the hands of Roman soldiers following a second failed Jewish revolt, but his knowledge of the many levels of the Bible lived on.

The trail of mysticism from this point to the twelfth century runs a ragged course. After the failure of the second revolt, Jews escaped and dispersed, spawning exile communities in many lands that would eventually be known as the Jewish Diaspora. The attention of Jewish leaders became less focused on spiritual matters and more focused on practical ones revolving around Jewish communal life. The second century to the sixth century C.E. became known as the Talmudic period, in which the revealed oral traditions and legends that had passed down through the generations since the revelations at Sinai were collected and written down. The painstaking process of debating, commenting on, and compiling all the traditions and legends involved hundreds of rabbis and unfolded over several centuries and several lands, culminating in the publication of the Babylonian Talmud around 500 C.E.

From the fifth century to the twelfth, Talmudic studies dominated Jewish theology, and mysticism took a back seat to the more pressing matters of managing the day-to-day life of the community. Mysticism didn't disappear during this period—there were still practitioners of it—it simply retreated to circles outside mainstream Jewish studies. Over the next centuries, Merkavah texts, some of which survive today, made their way quietly across the Mediterranean to Europe, and were circulating in Provence in the twelfth century when Kabbalah, the movement, began to take shape within the medieval Jewish community there.

KABBALAH IN THE MIDDLE AGES

The Middle Ages in Western Europe were characterized by religious and political fervor as well as by great intellectual activity in the Jewish, Christian, and Muslim communities. These were tumultuous times in Europe, and so much was going on in the areas of philosophy, theology, and science that it's no wonder Kabbalah found a life here among scholars who were as versed in the Torah as they were in the rational discussions of their age. Spain in particular was a beehive of Jewish intellectual growth during this period. The Jewish community there thrived under the Islamic rule of the moderate Spanish caliphate. Jews occupied important social positions and many Jewish philosophers, doctors, and mathematicians played leading roles in the development of medicine and science. They wrote volumes on medical remedies and ethics, invented navigation equipment, contributed advancements to geography and cartography, and translated into Arabic much of the Greek works on geometry, physics, and astronomy that would become the foundations for our later science. It was also a golden age for Jewish literature, marked by the emergence of great poets such as Judah Halevi and the noted twelfth- and thirteenth-century philosophers Moses ben Nahman (Nahmanides) and Moses ben Maimon (Maimonides), a leader of the school of rationalists who drew parallels between Aristotelian and Jewish thought and wrote the influential philosophical tome *Guide to the Perplexed* around 1191.

Mystical texts were circulating among elite circles at this time, and in France between 1150 and 1200 a manuscript appeared called *Sefer Ha Bahir* ("The Book of Brilliance"), which was a collection of mystical interpretations of the Bible. No one knows where the book originated—as with nearly all early mystical works, the author's identity remained a mystery—but the manuscript became known as the first official Kabbalist text. It was one of the first works to introduce the concept of other realities of existence beyond the comprehension of our physical senses. One person who was especially intrigued by the text was a man named Isaac the Blind, who would become the preeminent Kabbalist of his time.

It is unclear whether Isaac the Blind was truly blind (scholars argue that it would have been difficult for him to study the Torah as carefully as he did if he couldn't see it) or whether his name was merely a metaphor for the blinding spiritual light within him. It was said that he could sense the good and evil in a person's soul, as well as predict how long a person would live. While he wasn't a prolific Kabbalist—he only wrote a few works throughout his life—his influence on Kabbalah was significant.

Isaac the Blind was the first to use the name *kabbalah* with regard to the mystical teachings. He began to examine the story of Genesis and developed a theory about how the forces of God, the sefirot, evolved and interacted over time to create our universe and us in it. Anyone who reads his text will be amazed at how closely his seven-hundred-year-old writings resemble the most recent theories about the Big Bang and Reverse Big Bang. Rabbi Isaac also showed how humans evolved from God and were essentially a manifestation of the divine energy in the physical world. He used the words *Ein Sof* to denote God for the first time and put forth a theory of Creation as a process that went from Divine Will to thought to the utterance of words, through which the world was ultimately created. The Torah, he proposed, was the key to seeing our place in the universe, and was also the bridge to connecting our divine spirit back to God.

Partly due to his social status as son of the head of Provence's Jewish community, Rabbi Isaac's words carried enormous weight, and his disciples, who came from as far as Spain, carried his beliefs back to the Jewish communities in Gerona and Castile, where they began to take root in the latter twelfth and early thirteenth centuries. Isaac the Blind himself opposed the general dissemination of Kabbalah, but once in Spain, his ideas began to disperse to a wider audience and were embraced by a young Nachmanides, who would later become the top religious authority of Spain. There were still those who opposed Kabbalah as heresy, but the fact that a man of Nachmanides' stature could be a proponent of Kabbalah indicated for many that it was not far from traditional Judaism and that there was nothing to fear from it.

While the ideas of Kabbalah were taking shape during this time, they were still fairly obscure and passed hand to hand quietly from Kabbalah master to disciple. This began to change toward the end of the thirteenth century, when the *Sefer Ha Zohar* ("Book of Splendor") was published around 1280 in Spain, and became the seminal work of Kabbalah, its so-called bible after the Bible itself. The Zohar revealed the mysteries of Kabbalah to a whole new and wider audience. Ideas and interpretations that previously were fragmented and oblique became fully developed and linked in the Zohar.

SEFER HA ZOHAR—THE BOOK OF SPLENDOR

"Four Rabbis Were Riding Through the Galilee. . ."

This sounds like the beginning of a Jay Leno joke, but this summation is at least in part an accurate description of the Zohar as an account of a series of walking strolls or road trips embarked on by four rabbis who ride through the Galilee on donkeys, troubadour-style, espousing theories and stories about the Torah. Rabbi Shimon bar Yochai, a second-century master, is the protagonist of the book. He embarks on the journeys with Rabbi Yose, Rabbi Judah, and Rabbi Hiyya. Along the way, they meet Rabbi Phineas coming in the opposite direction and take leave of their mounts to settle in the shade of a tree to kibitz. During the course of their discussions, Rabbi Shimon tosses out biblical passages for his companions to interpret, as if playing some ancient form of Quiz Show. This, at least, is the surface structure that holds the book together.

Written in Aramaic, and divided into three parts with further subdivisions, it is a strange but wonderful book that has little form to it. The narrative has no linear structure but instead jumps back and forth, delivering information about such topics as the Creation of man, the nature of good and evil, and how our actions affect the destiny of the soul, all couched in stories, expositions, allegories, and little Zenlike koans. The story of Jonah and the whale, for instance, is explained in the Zohar as an allegory about the course a man's life takes in this world. The narrative of the book has elements of eroticism and Shakespearean comedy to it, as well as touches of a Carlos Castaneda story without the benefit of peyote. And all of it is very much colored by the personalities of the storytellers.

One night, for instance, when Rabbi Hiyya and Rabbi Yose meet, Rabbi Yose declares how great it is to be in Rabbi Hiyya's profound presence, after enduring the annoying company of his old and simpleton donkey driver who pestered him throughout his journey with all manner of foolish questions and tiring riddles, such as, What commences in union and ends up in separation? What are they who descend when they ascend, and ascend when they descend? Who is the beautiful virgin who has no eyes?

Rabbi Hiyya, curious about the fool's identity, summons him to appear before the two rabbis. When the old man appears, he begins to spout more gibberish but then reveals himself to be a learned man whose nonsensical riddles carry great insight. The two rabbis fall down before him weeping, and Rabbi Yose learns an invaluable lesson: Just as he shouldn't judge the Torah by its seemingly simple clothes (because there are wonderful secrets and messages hidden within it), so he shouldn't judge the fool (or the foolish experience for that matter), because he may also carry hidden lessons and wisdom. As Rabbi Hiyya concludes, sometimes "a seemingly hollow vessel holds some grains of gold."

The first part of the Zohar is composed of allegories that depict the nature and life of the soul. Shimon bar Yochai and his merry band of travelers make many appearances in this section. The second section, the main one, consists of a collection of writings that further explore the nature of God, the world, and the soul. In the final section, Rabbi Shimon carries on an imaginary conversation with Moses about the secrets embedded in the commandments. But while the parts imply that there is order to the narrative, there is actually no single adhesive to bind them. At one point we are offered what seem to be orderly interpretations of the five books of Moses. But then the work departs from this pattern and embarks on stream-of-consciousness flights of fancy to offer interpretations of the interpretations that seem to be written by a different author or authors.

As with *Sefer Ha Bahir,* the Zohar contends that buried within the words of the Torah are mysteries that can be uncovered with careful study. The Torah and Zohar deal with the same issues surrounding the relationship between humans and God, but whereas the Torah addresses the tangible, physical nature of that relationship—with regard to laws, behavior, and rituals—the Zohar elevates the relationship and issues to a spiritual plane. The Torah describes the physical picture of how the world was created, while the Zohar peaks behind the curtain to see the wizard in action, to see the turning wheels of the machinery of Creation.

The Zohar is the first book to deal with issues that until its time were only hinted at in the Torah. It crystallizes the theory of the sefirot and the emanation of the creating forces from God. The primary theme of the Zohar is that everything in the universe is connected—nothing is haphazard or random. It also sees Creation as an ongoing process, rather than a one-time incident with a static outcome. The process is governed by principles of cause and effect that influence the interaction between all parts of this interconnected universe, and behind this process there is a reason, indeed a purpose. The Zohar, an enormous work consisting of three volumes, has never been translated in its entirety, although a complete translation is currently in the works.

The ideas introduced in the Zohar helped open up a whole new way of reading the Torah. But despite its significance today, the book didn't really achieve prominence until nearly a hundred years after its appearance, due to a controversy that shadowed its publication. The author, Rabbi Moshe de Leon of Guadalajara, Spain, insisted that he didn't write the work. De Leon claimed that the author was really Rabbi Shimon bar Yochai, the book's leading character, who had lived in the second century C.E. and had been a disciple of the murdered Rabbi Akiva. After Akiva's death, bar Yochai had been forced to flee into the Galilean hills to escape Roman persecution; he settled in a cave there with his son for some thirteen years. There, de Leon claimed, the Prophet Elijah visited bar Yochai and revealed the ideas in the Zohar to him. The manuscript languished in a cave for centuries thereafter, de Leon claimed, until it was discovered by another Kabbalist who visited Palestine in the mid-thirteenth century and sent it back to Spain, where de Leon worked on it a number of years before publishing it.

The only problem with this story was that de Leon's witness, the Kabbalist whom he claimed found the manuscript, was dead. There was no one to confirm the story. Subsequently, a disciple of the dead Kabbalist appeared to say he'd never heard of the manuscript. He confronted de Leon, who invited the disciple back to his house in another town where he claimed to be

holding the original second-century manuscript. But before they
could return to de Leon's house, de Leon fell ill and died.

After de Leon's death, people came in search of the original
ancient manuscript, but de Leon's widow denied that such a
manuscript ever existed and insisted that the work was entirely
her husband's. Night after night, she said, he toiled on it alone.
The words belonged to him, not to some ancient Sanhedrin, she
insisted. Her husband only claimed it was written by bar Yochai
because he knew no one would care about his own work.

Some accused Mrs. de Leon of simply trying to garner recognition in death for a man who had never fully received it in life.
But most scholars agree with her version, since the writing style
of the Zohar is very much a product of the period in which it
was published. They conclude that de Leon either wrote the
Zohar himself or synthesized ideas that were circulating at the
time and ascribed the writing to bar Yochai simply to lend it
more authority—as was the custom of many authors in earlier
times who dealt with mystical or controversial ideas.

The fact that the Zohar was clouded in controversy didn't
make it less valuable or important. Although it wasn't the only
book of its kind at the time, it caught the attention of a small
group of devotees who felt it articulated precisely their views.
As the decades passed and the controversy over the Zohar's
publication faded, the number of its adherents grew. Although
Jewish leaders would later denounce it as a book of lies, for the
next three centuries, until the 1800s, the Zohar was regarded

with the highest esteem, equal to that of the Torah and Talmud. It was during this period that the study of Kabbalah really began to take root and grow.

Not everyone in the Jewish community welcomed the Kabbalists' queries and speculations about God and Creation, however. Mainstream Jewish leaders began to fear that Kabbalah would lead people astray and prevent them from studying and practicing traditional Judaism. Already weary of Jewish assimilation, the leaders feared Kabbalah would take people away from the synagogue and cause them to forget the commandments. Kabbalists were divided between those who sought to restrict its teachings to select disciples and those who sought to spread the secrets to as many people as possible. In general, the study of Kabbalah was restricted to men who already had a strong grounding in Torah studies. This, of course, eliminated women entirely, as they were not allowed into the circle of holy studies.

One might wonder why Kabbalah emerged at the time it did. Why, if Kabbalah was based on the Bible, which had been around for centuries, didn't it develop long before the twelfth century? There are two responses to this that are connected: a Kabbalist response and a historian's response, both of which we touched on previously. The Kabbalist response is that everything is revealed in its time; that every generation receives its share of the Torah as the Torah reveals itself anew to each generation. But this idea that a generation receives only what it's ready to receive is also tied to history and the evolution of ideas that create an environment ripe for a generation to accept certain ideas. Scientific advancements do not occur overnight. They require years of study and small steps made by many people before one scientist makes a "discovery." Many minds and many people contribute to the final breakthrough, but it's only the one who dots the *i* who gets the final credit. The messages of Kabbalah always existed in the Bible, but it took the evolution of thought throughout the ages to create an environment in which the words of the Bible could be interpreted with deeper meaning. It took advancements in Jewish thought brought on by the Talmudic period and all the mystical, philosophic, and scientific writings that emerged over the centuries to form fully the images and ideas the Kabbalists were receiving.

Kabbalah may have also been a spiritual response to the rationalism of the age, propounded by Maimonides and others. The Kabbalists were devout and pious Jews who were restless for answers about Creation and God that traditional Jewish practice couldn't satisfy. Life had to be more than just a set of laws learned by rote and performed from sunup to sundown, they believed. On the other hand, the Kabbalists listened to what the rationalists were saying and sensed a profound absence of God. Kabbalah offered the possibility of an intimacy with God that intellectual Judaism couldn't provide. As Gershom Scholem has put it, it emerged at the intersection where tradition met intuition, where the concrete met the esoteric and the rational met the irrational. It was the result of a great urge to get at the essence of the Torah and experience God in a new way. Kabbalists were delving into issues of existentialism and asking new and daring questions that hadn't been proposed before. They went beyond the early mystics, who saw themselves as being apart from God without asking why the separation occurred. The Kabbalists wondered if Creation occurred for a reason, if humans were created for a purpose; and if yes, then they wanted to know what that purpose was.

Perhaps another reason for Kabbalah's emergence during the Middle Ages was related to the social condition of the Jews at the time. While the beginning of the Middle Ages had been a golden age for European Jewry, the end of the eleventh century, when *Sefer Ha Bahir* began circulating, marked a quick and drastic end to those happier times. It began in 1096 with the first of the Christian Crusades, which ultimately led to the demise of the Spanish caliphate and the takeover of more orthodox Muslim dynasties from Morocco, resulting in various forms of persecution for Jews over the next 400 years. The Christians in Spain eventually ousted the Islamic empire altogether, thus beginning a long period of systematic persecution of the Jewish people, which culminated in 1492, the year Columbus set sail on his momentous voyage. Jews were expelled from influential posts and forced to convert or were tortured and burnt at the stake. In 1109 the Jewish communities of Grenada and Toledo were massacred, and in 1171, in France, the first blood libel case emerged, in which Jews were accused of killing a missing Christian child and using its blood for ritual purposes. Some 100,000 Jews were expelled from Spain and forced to relocate to North Africa and the eastern Mediterranean. Along with this dispersed population the ideas of Kabbalah spread, and the study of this mystical trend became even more available to the masses.

MODERN KABBALIST THOUGHT

During the mid-sixteenth century, a new and bustling center of Kabbalah study emerged first in Jerusalem, then settled in the tiny northern Galilean town of Safed, which remains to this day a small Kabbalist enclave. Here, the final most significant events in the development of Kabbalah occurred with the teachings of Rabbis Moshe Cordovero and Isaac Luria, the fathers of modern Kabbalist thought.

Moshe Cordovero lived in the mid-1500s in Safed, where he was a devoted and gifted scholar of the revealed Torah. He was so gifted that he was a bit of a prodigy and was ordained a rabbi at the age of eighteen. Two years after he became a rabbi, Cordovero began studying the hidden Torah with his wife's brother, Solomon Alkabetz, a noted Kabbalist, and it wasn't long before Cordovero became a leading Kabbalist himself.

In Safed, Cordovero lived within a circle of extremely pious men, who held themselves to a high ideal of asceticism and morality in which they sought to banish angry and evil thoughts from their minds. They spent their days in deep contemplation, developing interpretations of the Kabbalist texts, particularly the Zohar, which was printed for the first time in 1558 and distributed widely throughout Europe. Ultimately, Cordovero composed a massive text of his own, a compendium of Jewish mysticism that categorized all the principles of Kabbalah, as well as some thirty manuscripts of his own teachings, which included an introduction to Kabbalah, a book of ethics based on the ten sefirot, and a massive volume that is considered one of the most comprehensive commentaries on the Zohar. His book of ethics, *The Tree of Devorah,* became extremely popular among sixteenth-century Kabbalists and, aside from some dated and chauvinistic viewpoints, is still relevant today, particularly as it relates to practical Kabbalah and our daily life. Cordovero's writings helped synthesize and summarize Kabbalah up to the sixteenth century, and his work influenced many people, including Spinoza. He became a legend in his own time and attracted many disciples who later wrote their own books based on his ideas. When he died in 1570 at the age of forty-eight, it was reported that a pillar of fire appeared at his coffin.

The study of Kabbalah changed Cordovero's life. In fact, despite the many years of learning that preceded his study of the hidden Torah, he wrote that once he began to study Kabbalah it was as if his entire life he'd been asleep. Kabbalah made him a fully aware and conscious being.

Isaac Luria, also known as the ARI, an acronym for his Hebrew title (Ha Elohi Rabbi Yitzhak—The Divine Rabbi Isaak) studied in Safed with Moshe Cordovero a year before Cordovero died. If Cordovero was important for the structured development of Kabbalah, the ARI was essential for contemporizing Kabbalah and clarifying its principles. Luria meditated on the Zohar and was said to receive revelations from the Prophet Elijah, which he then incorporated into his teachings. He refined and reshaped the Tree of Life and made the mystical teachings more accessible.

During his short lifetime, Luria attracted many would-be disciples. But he guarded his teachings fiercely and carefully selected his students. Oddly enough, he never wrote his teachings down. One of his students put them in writing after his death. Although his life was short—he lived only three years in Safed before he died in an epidemic at the age of thirty-eight, a factor that led to his mythologization—Luria's innovative ideas, along with Cordovero's contributions, ultimately helped define and systematize Kabbalah, and it is mainly his ideas, known as the Lurianic tradition, that form the basis of most Kabbalah teaching and writing today.

The period of Safed represented the golden era of Kabbalah studies, and from around 1630, Lurianic Kabbalah began to spread from Persia to North Africa to Italy and Eastern Europe, perhaps due in part to the availability of the texts with the advent of printing. Kabbalah during this period was highly regarded and actually dominated Jewish studies and teachings throughout the Middle East and most of Europe. In Safed and many other places, there was no separation between ordinary Torah and Talmud studies and the study of Kabbalah; those who studied the Torah and Talmud also studied Kabbalah. For the first time in history, the revealed and hidden Torahs stood side by side. But it was the first and last time, according to Kabbalah scholar Gershom Scholem, that a unified Jewish theology would exist. Beginning in 1666, while Kabbalah would still retain high stature, unity in the Jewish community would begin to dissolve, and Jewish history after that would be a story of fractious enmity and division.

THE END OF UNITY

During the seventeenth century, the situation for Jews in Eastern Europe—Poland and the Ukraine especially—declined dramatically as it had earlier in Spain. Anti-Semitism ballooned in Prague with more blood libel claims, in which Jews were accused of slaughtering Christian children to use their blood to make matzoh bread for Passover, and these accusations spread to the Ukraine, where Jews from Poland had settled among resentful Cossacks. Intense persecution culminated in 1648 and 1649 in the pogroms of the Cossacks, in which entire Jewish populations were exterminated or driven off the land. Some 300 Jewish towns and villages were destroyed and more than

100,000 Jews killed. It was a grave time for Jewish leaders. The communities were deeply affected by these events and felt abandoned by the learned men who spent their days bent over books but couldn't save the community or provide adequate answers for why they were suffering. As a result, Judaism was thrust into a deep spiritual crisis. Disillusioned by traditional Judaism, many people seeking spiritual and political redemption found hope in Kabbalah, which claimed that prayer could bring about repair of the world and redemption. A system that was traditionally contemplative in nature began to transform into one that offered messages of hope. Furthermore, people found in Lurianic Kabbalah signs that the world was indeed nearing the final stages of redemption, and with these ideas, Messianic fervor began to take root.

It was perhaps inevitable that out of this climate someone would emerge who offered the Jews in exile salvation and redemption. This at least was their hope about Shabbetai Zvi, the false messiah mentioned in chapter 1. Zvi was born in Smyrna (Izmir, Turkey today) in 1626 and came of age around the time of the pogroms. He came from a wealthy family and was an exceptionally gifted and devoted scholar who became a member of the rabbinical elite. But he was also an extremely eccentric loner and suffered what today would be considered episodes of manic-depression that would produce erratic behavior. Out of the blue he would begin uttering the unmentionable name of God in public squares and advocated abolishing the commandments of

Judaism. Not surprisingly, the rabbis of Smyrna kicked him out of the community, after which he settled in Jerusalem.

For years he struggled with the demons inside him. He married twice, but the unions were never consummated and ended in divorce. He finally married a woman who was rumored to be a prostitute. Everything in his life culminated in his meeting in the mid-1660s with a man named Nathan Ashkenazi, who had visions of Zvi as the Messiah. Ashkenazi showed Zvi writings that seemed to suggest the Messiah would be named Shabbetai and be born on Zvi's birthdate. Zvi deduced from this that he was indeed the Messiah and made a formal announcement in Gaza in 1665. The news spread swiftly throughout the Middle East and Europe, arousing a Messianic fervor around him and legends of his apparent ability to perform miracles. He attracted thousands of devotees throughout Europe and created frenzied anticipation among the despairing communities there who were waiting for someone to release them from their suffering. They sold their businesses and belongings and awaited a signal from the Messiah to return to the Holy Land. This atmosphere of anticipation continued for nearly a year before the Ottoman authorities grew alarmed by the thought of thousands of ecstatic Jews converging on the Ottoman-controlled holy city, and arrested Zvi on charges of sedition. Five months later they gave him a choice: conversion to Islam or death. Amazingly, Zvi chose conversion, and even changed his name to Aziz. While some of his adherents were shocked into reality by the idea of the Messiah becoming Muslim, others asserted that it must be part of the Messianic plan and followed Zvi into Islam. For some time after his conversion, a movement continued of radical Shabbatean Kabbalists, who distorted the teachings of Kabbalah and reasoned that if all things were divine as the Kabbalists said they were, then sin was divine too. They engaged in orgies and all manner of heresy until they were forced underground. Fringes of them survived until the early twentieth century, and Messianism itself continued in various forms for many years thereafter. But Zvi himself lived out the remainder of his life off a small pension from the Ottoman coffers and died on Yom Kippur in 1676 at the age of fifty.

The despair and shock felt by many Jews in the aftermath of the Zvi debacle led many of them back to traditional rabbinical Judaism, which, from that time on, dominated normative Jewish learning up to the present day. Kabbalah experienced another resurgence, though of a different nature, with the founding of modern Hassidism in the Ukraine in the eighteenth century. Rabbi Israel ben Eliezer, also known as the Baal Shem Tov (Master of the Good Name, because it was said that he possessed the secret knowledge of God's name) was born around 1700 and became a healer and charismatic mystic who witnessed the suffering of the communities in Europe and sought to find a solution to the spiritual crisis within Judaism. He began to study Kabbalah and came to the conclusion that the intellectual masters in Safed had it all wrong. If everything in this world was created by God, then we should celebrate that Creation, rather than vilify it by living an austere and somber life. The Kabbalists in Safed believed that the more rooted in the physical they were, the less spiritual they would be. Eliezer, believed the opposite. Instead of removing ourselves from the physical world, he taught that we should celebrate it as God's creation, but all the while he practiced strict adherence to orthodox Judaism.

The Hassidim today continue to practice a combination of orthodoxy with strong mystical undertones, adhering particularly to the belief that everything in the physical world has a spark of the divine in it and is therefore worthy of awe. But while the Hassidim adopted many of the ideas espoused by Kabbalists, they have always held firmly to traditional Judaism, relegating Kabbalah to an avocational position that exists mainly to support the precepts of the commandments and Jewish law. In general, they tend not to delve too deeply into the cosmic layers of Kabbalah, and we should not confuse modern Hassidim with true Kabbalists, although many of the Kabbalists of the last three centuries have also been Hassidim.

As Kabbalah began to fade in mainstream circles over the years, the Hassidim have kept its flame alive, preserving its teachings throughout the nineteenth and twentieth centuries. During World War II, Kabbalah received another blow when an entire lineage of Kabbalist scholars disappeared in Nazi concentration camps. With the passing and collapse of communities that held Kabbalah and the Book of Zohar in high esteem, the belief system quietly disappeared for many years. In Europe, the study of Kabbalah declined for the most part during the nineteenth century, and took a back seat to normative Jewish studies and practices that focused on Jewish law and ritual rather than the cosmic oneness of the world.

It has only been in the last twenty years that a new generation of Jews and non-Jews has been rediscovering and reviving the teachings, mostly the Lurianic tradition of Kabbalah, and finding the words very much applicable to our modern and complex times.

three

SOME KEY PRINCIPLES
OF KABBALAH

A NONLINEAR SYSTEM

Before we discuss some of the key principles of Kabbalah, it will be helpful to mention a few things. Kabbalah, for one, is not a linearly organized belief system. The system is many-layered and interwoven like a ball of string that is composed, instead of a single strand, of many, many strands wrapped tightly around one another. One principle segues into another and then another, and it is difficult to discuss one aspect of Kabbalah without going off on tangents to cover others. But despite its complexity, when broken down and evaluated Kabbalah offers a surprisingly sensible and congruent view of our place in the scheme of things.

For instance, we could talk about the significance of the number seven in the Book of Genesis, and we would have to draw a complex tree to include all the ways in which the number appears throughout Kabbalah and traditional Jewish history. In

Kabbalah, the seven days of Creation (including the day of rest) are metaphors for seven of the forces of God that are responsible for Creation, which are depicted by seven of the spheres on the Tree of Life, the primary symbol of Kabbalah. (There are actually ten spheres on the Tree, but humans are capable of comprehending only seven of them; the other three, however, are implied in Genesis.) What's more, early mystics said there were seven levels to the realm of heaven, and Kabbalists say that we are now in the seventh cycle of Creation; that prior to the time recorded in Genesis, there were six other cycles of Creation.

But this is just seven as it appears on the esoteric level. There is also the mundane level. The seven days of Creation in Genesis also become the seven days of the week that put order into our lives; in Jewish tradition, seven is the number of days that family and friends sit in mourning for the dead; the seventh year in Judaism is a sabbatical year, when agricultural fields are supposed to lay fallow, when leased or sold land returns to its owner, and when slaves are freed and debts repaid.

Each of these examples has its own explanation and reasoning behind it, and each practice and belief is connected in some obvious or esoteric way to the greater scheme of Creation. The Kabbalists made it their mission to find these connections and give proof to the idea that there is order at all levels of the universe. The result is that there is essentially no end to Kabbalah. The universe runs on synchronicity, and once you begin to study Kabbalah, you begin to see its principles cropping up everywhere and in everything. It is the undercurrent pulsing throughout the universe.

The majority of Kabbalist writings focus on the Creation story, on describing how Creation unfolded. This is because it is mainly through the story of Creation that we come to "know" God, that God reveals aspects of Himself or gives us hints as to who He is and who we are in relation to Him. Throughout the Kabbalists' discourses on the events of Creation, however, they examine numerous other subjects, such as the nature and characteristics of God and the nature of humans and the soul. From these three topics—Creation, God, and humans—Kabbalists arrive at an understanding about our inner feelings and emotions and the nature of our human relationships. They address issues such as greed and jealousy, pride and humility, charity and lust, even the care and nurturing of a child; and it is at these levels that Kabbalah is brought into practice. Within the story of Creation is not only a model for understanding the universe but for understanding ourselves as well.

As with all complex systems of thought, some theories and aspects of Kabbalah are more developed than others. There are also important questions for which the Kabbalists fail to supply adequate answers; there are others that they simply ignore altogether. But there is so much that they do address that it would be ungracious of us to complain. What's more, Kabbalists did not arrive at their concepts arbitrarily. The ideas expressed here are the result of decades and centuries of contemplation and study by some of the most advanced minds at work in the Middle Ages.

However, when we say "Kabbalists believe" or "according to Kabbalists," we are not talking about a group of unified minds. Different Kabbalists throughout the centuries have focused on different aspects of Creation and supplied different interpretations and symbols for their readings of Genesis. Some Kabbalists, for example, believe that the Book of Genesis can be viewed as a meditation guide for attaining closeness to God; others see in the story of Creation an intellectual process involving the evolution of thoughts and ideas into action through language and speech; others see Creation as a kind of de-evolution or stepping-down process of the God force, and they describe God as light and picture Him "pouring" Himself or His light into the world.

All of these are valid readings. Remember, there are seventy faces to the Torah, and more than one of these faces is a Kabbalist face. But as we said previously, this does not present a case for contradictions; instead it leads us to a basic Kabbalah concept about the Torah: There is no right or wrong answer. All interpretations are plausible. It is not a question of one or the other; Genesis has many possible readings, all of which lead us to a fuller understanding of the message within it. While the specific language and symbolism of the Kabbalists may differ, they are all describing the same phenomenon: the Creation of our universe by a force that originated in God. Whether the Kabbalists describe that force as a process of God dividing

Himself, pouring Himself, or sending divine thoughts into the vast space doesn't really matter. All Kabbalist paths lead to the same conclusion: that Creation is an ongoing event and that there is a reason behind it.

I begin this description of Kabbalah with a few key concepts, to define some of the terms and ideas, and then show how they figure in the Kabbalist understanding of Creation. This will provide a broad view of how the Kabbalists believe the universe was formed as well as explain their ideas for why we are here.

In grappling with the principles of Kabbalah, however, we must understand that our vocabulary isn't up to par with some of the concepts we are discussing. Some terminology might seem inelegant or inadequate. The Kabbalists are dealing with concepts that are, quite literally, difficult to conceptualize. They don't have adequate language to describe these ideas, so they resort to words and descriptions that make the best sense. For instance, the Kabbalists describe God in ways that make Him seem human; they ascribe mortal qualities and emotions to Him—God "thinks" this, and "feels" that. This is not done in traditional Judaism, which frowns on assigning human characteristics to God. (This is one of the reasons why there are no paintings or statues of God in Judaism or Jewish art.) The purpose is not only to avoid the idolization of images, but also to acknowledge that God is beyond our comprehension. God is not human, and to depict Him in the figure of a person is to make Him mundane, to put flesh on something that is not flesh.

The Kabbalists get around this infraction, however, by re-peating over and over again that what they are describing is not God Himself, but aspects of Him. This leads us to our first principle.

GOD CANNOT BE KNOWN

It is understood in Kabbalah that some things will never be known. Some things are beyond our comprehension as human beings. Who created the universe, however, is not one of them. About this, the Kabbalists don't quibble: God created the uni-verse and everything in it.

But just who God is, or what God is, is undefinable. One of the first principles of Kabbalah, then, is that God cannot be known. This is fairly ironic, since all of Kabbalah is based on the impulse to know God and to understand His powers.

We *can* know God to a certain degree, the Kabbalists say; we can know some of the characteristics or aspects or parts of God that He reveals to us, but beyond these we are handicapped by our human limitations. We belong to the finite world, and God belongs to the world of the infinite, which is beyond our human comprehension. Any attempt to know Him, to define who or what He is, puts boundaries on the infinite, which essentially negates its infiniteness. Kabbalists liken this to trying to catch a thought in the palm of your hand. It cannot be done.

How do we know something? By defining it and by giving it a name; by describing what characteristics belong to it and then by assigning those characteristics names. Any animal that is warm-blooded, has vertebrae, mammary glands, and hair is given the name of *mammal*. We know it by the characteristics it has, and then we combine all of this information into a code (a name) which becomes shorthand for the thing itself.

Another way we know a thing is to distinguish it from what it is not. In other words, when we see a bird and don't know what kind of bird it is, we first eliminate everything that it is not. In the same way, we might try to approach God by defining Him by what He is not; only we don't get very far because there isn't anything that God is not. God is everything, so to assign Him a name would be to say that He is this, but He is not that. This we cannot do, because there is no end to what God is and what God includes. God, the congruence of all things past, present, and future, the representation of all time and no time at the same time, is within His essence unlimited, and if unlimited then undefinable, and if undefinable then unnamable, and if unnamable then ultimately unknowable.

This is why when religious Jews write the name of God in English, they spell it *G-d,* as a way to acknowledge that God cannot be captured by language, and why when Jews reading the Bible aloud come across the traditional four-letter name for God in Hebrew—*YHWH* (also known as "the Tetragrammaton," from the Greek word for "four letters")—they substitute the names *Elohim* or *Adonai* instead, which are less sacred names for God. God has a name—after all, we have to refer to him by something—but we cannot speak it.

YHWH is called "the Ineffable Name of God." The infiniteness of God is actually expressed in this name. YHWH is a conglomeration of the past, present, and future conjugations of the Hebrew verb "to be." God is all things and all places and time. He has no beginning—as far as we can determine—and He has no end—as far as we assume. He just is; or rather He was, is, and always will be. When all the Hebrew letters of the conjugations for "it was," "it is," and "it will be" are joined and double letters removed, we are left with the Hebrew letters *yud-heh-vav-heh,* which is unpronounceable as a word.

Some people have tried to pronounce it as "Yahweh" or "Jehovah." But it is said that only the ancient Jewish High Priest in the Temple in Jerusalem knew how to say God's name, and he was only allowed to utter it one day a year, on Yom Kippur. One writer, Arthur Waskow, has suggested that the pronunciation of it is *Yhewoooo,* the sound of breath; which is an elegant idea—that God, the giver of life, is represented by the sound of life-giving breath. This recalls a poignant Jewish legend I read years ago, which states that before an infant is born, its soul stands before God and is given the secrets of the universe and Creation. But just before the child leaves its mother, an angel follows it to the womb and takes back the secrets, leaving the child in anguish. When the newborn takes its first shuddering breath and cries, it is really uttering the name of God, crying out at being separated from Him and having lost the knowledge of Him.

THE WORLD WAS CREATED
VIA TEN EMANATIONS FROM GOD

With the statement that God cannot be known, and thus named, comes what would seem to be the first Kabbalist contradiction, because the Kabbalists do in fact give God a name—*Ein Sof*. But this name is simply a kind of placeholder that only further emphasizes the fact that we cannot fence in the concept of God. *Ein Sof* in Hebrew means "without end," so rather than naming God, the Kabbalists give a name to the idea that God cannot be named.

The name *Ein Sof* never appears anywhere in the Bible. Instead, the Bible mentions ten other names for God: Ehiyeh Asher Ehiyeh, Yah, YHWH (Elohim or Adonai), El, Elohim, Adonai Tzevaot, Elohim Tzevaot, Shaddai, Adonai, and El Chai. (The names inside parentheses indicate what should be vocalized instead of YHWH, when reading aloud.) In the English version of the Bible, of course, all of these Hebrew names are simply translated as God, or sometimes as Yahweh or Jehovah; there is no indication that the name keeps changing in the original.

According to Kabbalists, these ten variations actually represent distinguishable characteristics of Ein Sof, not Ein Sof Himself. They are attributes of Ein Sof that He emanates from Himself, in order to create the universe. These ten forces that created and continue to sustain the universe are called "sefirot" by Kabbalists. Each one of these sefirot has a God name; any time one of these names appears in the text of the Bible, particularly in the Book of Genesis, it is simply to tell us that that particular aspect of God is manifesting or acting at that time. God's real name, Ein Sof, never appears in the Bible because He exists in a realm above and beyond the realm of the sefirot, in an unlimited realm that is incomprehensible to us. The sefirot are the closest we can come to knowing God.

The concept of the sefirot is similar to the relationship between me and my creative talents. Let's say I have a knack for photography. You can say that this talent is a part of me, but it is not me in my entirety. It is only one aspect of me that I carry inside. I have other creative aspects too: the artist in me draws pictures; the cook in me prepares meals; the writer in me writes an article. All of these are aspects of me, but each one alone is not me. All of them together make up that one part of me that I would call my creative talents. But there are other parts to me as well. There are the parts that make up my personality, such as feelings and emotions, memories and experiences. There are parts that make up my relationships: daughter, sister, lover, friend. And there are the external parts that make up the part of me that the

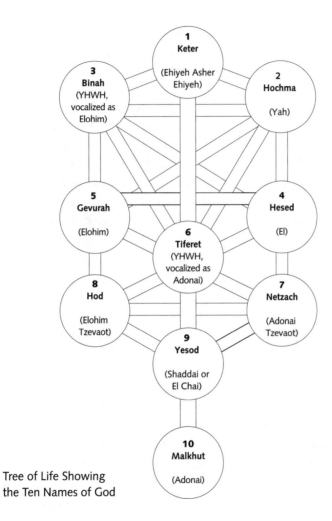

Tree of Life Showing
the Ten Names of God

world sees at first glance: my physical appearance, mannerisms, and way of speaking. All of these are parts of who I am.

Now let's say I create a being that consists of all of my creative talents only, a selective cloning perhaps; and this being further divides itself into separate beings that represent each individual talent, and these beings together proceed to create something, each contributing the unique talent that defines it. I am still me, but I have focused a certain aspect of myself to accomplish a task. In the same way, God created an aspect of Himself to accomplish Creation, and this aspect was formed of ten forces depicted as the sefirot on the Kabbalist Tree of Life.

CREATION BEGAN WITH
THE CONTRACTION OF GOD

As one of the first acts of Creation, Kabbalists say, God withdrew from Himself to form a finite space for our universe. Put broadly, billions of years ago, the idea of Creation came to God (or rather the idea formed "inside" of Him) and He set about putting the idea into action through a series of steps, which involved first the contraction of Himself and then the emanation from Him of an energy force composed of seven forces (sefirot) that would serve as the agents or actors of all Creation.

Here's how Kabbalists describe what happened:

In the beginning of the beginning, there was only Ein Sof, who was represented by white light, which was everywhere and everything. The light that was Ein Sof filled everything. There were no empty or black spaces, just white, unrefracted, and unlimited light that irradiated everywhere. There was no beginning to this light, and no end. There was nothing outside of Ein Sof; there was only Ein Sof, which represented singular unity and oneness.

When the idea to create the world arose in the will of Ein Sof, He withdrew Himself from part of Himself to create a space for Creation to exist in; that is, He created a point of blackness, a vacuum in the center of His light, in order to create a space for Creation. It was only a very small space that He created, a "point" as Kabbalists describe it; but size is relative. Compared to the vast infinity that Ein Sof encompassed, the black space that He created for our universe was indeed a tiny point.

Since God encompasses everything, since He is everything, He had to create a space in which He didn't exist in order to create something that would be distinct from him. We can liken it to an architect clearing off his drafting table to create a working space. In Kabbalist language, what God did was create a space in which to create the universe by "removing" Himself from that space, by creating a "hole," or a kind of nothingness or empty place in which He didn't exist.

Kabbalists call the creation of the black space the *tzimtzum.* *Keter,* the first sefira on the Tree of Life, represents this act of contraction. Keter is the darkness, the nothingness. Ein Sof creates this empty space by drawing Himself in or collapsing in on Himself. The result is blackness, which is a space in which the Light of God has regressed. The process of contraction can be compared to a cone. Light is drained or sucked into the cone, and then something emanates back out of the cone. It is as if God sucked in a part of the light that was Him, and then blew out a smaller stream of it. The black space created is at the center of the universe and into this space the emanation is sent. Recall that Arthur Waskow suggested that the name of God, YHWH, is the sound of breath. God "breathes" the letters of his name into the emptiness to create the universe. He breathes life into the universe. It is said in the Zohar that "without the soul-breath, the body could not conduct itself, would not be aware of the Will, could not actualize the Will of the Creator."

The description is surprisingly similar to that of a black hole. A black hole is a place where the laws of physics as we know them today do not apply, a place in which what is believed to be a star collapses in on itself because its nuclear fuel is depleted and no longer balances the gravitational force. It's a space in which the gravitational force of an extreme concentration of mass causes light to be trapped inside rather than being emitted. Of course we can't know for certain if this is what happened scientifically, but it's amazing to think that thirteenth-century Kabbalists, through their meditations, may have tapped into a phenomenon that wasn't introduced by science until well into the twentieth century.

Once the black space was created, God poured a measured dose of His energy back into it. He sent out an emanation, a stream of pure, white light, into the center of the darkness or black space. Say, for instance, you lay a sheet of white paper onto a table and you cut a round hole in the center of it, an empty space in which there is no paper. But then you take the circle that you removed and you cut it into several small, white stars, and you sprinkle the stars onto the hole in the middle of the paper. You have created a space in the paper in which to place something else made out of the same material as that which you took out of the space. In the same way, God created a space by removing or withdrawing Himself, then poured Himself back into that space.

The white light descended into the center of the black space but remained connected to its source at the same time. Kabbalists call this stream the *Ein Sof Or,* the light of Ein Sof. This stream represents the pure, unrefracted "white" light of Ein Sof. The light is white because this is the color that is composed of all other colors and yet is no color itself. Refract white light through a prism and the colors within it become separated out from the white light. In the same way, the Ein Sof Or is composed of various aspects (the sefirot) of Ein Sof. Undifferentiated, they form white light; but as they are refracted, they separate out like the colors of light through a prism. The act of emanation from Ein Sof into the blackness is represented by the second sefira on the Tree, called *Hochma.*

Note that the initial step of Creation was a kind of dance of opposite movements. God emptied and then filled; He regressed into Himself and then sent forward a stream of Himself. As we will see later, this established an important precedent for Kabbalists with regard to spiritual evolution. The idea of taking one step back (an act of harsh judgment and self-limitation) and then many steps forward (an act of mercy and compassion) led Kabbalists to the concepts of sinning and making mistakes as steps toward redemption and renewal.

Through the interaction of the emanation with the darkness—the interaction between the first and the second sefira (Keter and Hochma)—the third sefira, *Binah,* emerges at the tip of the emanated light. Binah is the "mother" of all lower sefirot. From Binah, the remaining sefirot emerge, one after the other, one out of the other, like Russian nesting dolls. Each sefira on the Tree of Life becomes a vessel for God's energy as it emanates from Ein Sof, in an act that mirrors the original emanation into the black space. Each sefira plays a role in Creation, as the energy from Ein Sof flows through it and mixes with the qualities and elements therein to create something new that is passed to the next sefira and the next level. Think of a champagne tower at a wedding reception, with the glasses stacked in a pyramid. Champagne is poured into the glass on top until it overflows the glass and cascades down to the next level where it fills the next two glasses and cascades down to the third, and so on.

So, we have the all-encompassing white light; then the blackness; then the emanation of light into the blackness; and the end point of that emanation is the third sefira, which produces all other sefirot and, with them, our world. The force of God, at the point of Binah, the third sefira, breaks itself down from the all-encompassing one to the many, and forms the next seven sefirot, which consist of opposing powers and their balancing force. Our mind can only conceive of the lower seven sefirot. Beyond these, into the boundless light, we cannot know.

At each one of these stages on its way down from the upper spiritual realms to the lower and denser physical one, the pure form of energy or light that emanates from Ein Sof is "reduced" or refracted until finally the property produced is matter, our physical world. It's a bit like boiling a pot of river water. When the water is evaporated, what you are left with is the denser particles—the minerals—that cannot be carried by the lighter particles of steam.

There are other ways the Kabbalists depict the Creation process. Instead of depicting it as a flow of energy, they also describe it as a vast, never-ending source of water that divides into seven separate streams; or as the process of an idea evolving into thought and action. In this latter version, first there emerges within the Ein Sof the will or urge to create. Kabbalists call this the divine will and associate it with the sefira Keter. Once the will exists, it manifests itself in a thought in order to be recognized as existing at all. Kabbalists associate this thought stage with the second sefira, Hochma. Once the thought is created, the mind has to identify it, name it, determine its content and moral value, and begin to act on it. This is the sefira of Binah, in which differentiation occurs. (Is it a good idea or a bad idea? If it's a good idea, then what do I need to do in order to make it real?) The idea is named and begins to take shape. Now that we have a name for it, we can begin to create it. The remainder of the sefirot represent the process of actualizing or manifesting the original will to create.

It might seem that will and thought are the same thing, that the thought to move is basically the will to move. But science tells us otherwise. Take, for example, the simple act of moving your leg. Let's say your leg has been in a certain position for a while and is beginning to fall asleep, so you move it. But before you actually move it, you have the idea or thought to move it (of which you may not even be consciously aware), which signals your muscles to "move leg." Some people might say that the thought to move is the beginning of the process. But even before you think about moving your leg, something deeper inside you has willed the thought itself in your subconscious. Scientists in the 1960s discovered this with a now-famous experiment in which they implanted electrodes into subjects in the part of their brain that was responsible for the movement of limbs. The subjects were seated at a slide machine and told to watch the slides and advance the carousel by pushing a remote button. The button, however, did not actually control the advancement of the slides at all. Instead, a signal from the subjects' brain passed through the electrodes to a mechanism that then advanced the slides before the subjects could push the button, indeed, before they were even aware that they wanted to push the button. The projector seemed to operate outside of the subjects' control and "anticipate" what they wanted to do before they made the decision to do it. Scientists thus concluded that somewhere in our brain a will exists that knows what we are going to do before we are conscious of it and have a thought to do it. This is Keter.

THE UNIVERSE CONSISTS OF FOUR WORLDS

Kabbalists believe that our universe is composed of four worlds, four levels of Creation: our physical world and three others that are located between us and the source. These four worlds represent four phases through which the process of Creation passed from the act of *tzimtzum* to the final product, our physical world. The four, starting with the top one, nearest Ein Sof, are called:

1 Atzilut (the World of Emanation)

2 Briyah (the World of Creation)

3 Yetzirah (the World of Formation)

4 Assiyah (the World of Manifestation)

Atzilut, the world of emanation, represents the process in which *tzimtzum* occurred and the white light emanated from Ein Sof into the darkness. This is the closest world to Ein Sof,

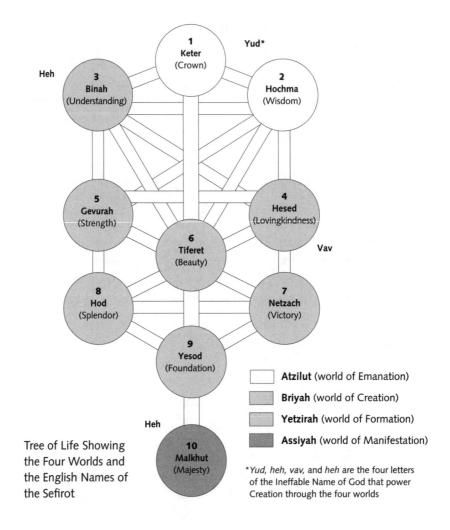

Tree of Life Showing
the Four Worlds and
the English Names of
the Sefirot

but it is not Ein Sof. Atzilut is different from the other three worlds because it still belongs to the realm of unity and oneness. *Briyah,* the world of creation, represents the stage from which the forces of God begin to emerge as opposites, balanced by equalizing powers. *Yetzirah,* the world of formation, represents the stage of activity in which things begin to take shape through the interaction of the sefirot and the flowing energy of Ein Sof. And finally, *Assiyah,* the world of manifestation, represents the physical world, the final product of all this activity.

Each of the four worlds is represented by one of the letters of the Tetragrammaton—YHWH. Atzilut is *yud* (Y); Briyah is *heh* (H); Yetzirah is *vav* (W); and Assiyah is the final *heh* (H). This means that the sacred four-letter name of God is the propelling force of Creation. It is the secret of the structure of the whole universe. Each of the four letters represents a different strain of energy involved in moving Creation from inception to manifestation. To speak the name of God, Kabbalists believe, is to conjure the forces of Creation. But remember, no one knows quite how to pronounce it.

Yud is the stage of emanation. The flow of energy emerges from Ein Sof as *yud* into the darkness, where it begins to create order in the chaos. *Yud* organizes the chaos of the *tzimtzum* to produce Binah, from which the lower sefirot emerge and actual creation begins. Within Binah, a second force, *heh,* comes into play, which causes Binah to become impregnated with the remainder of the sefirot and "give birth" to the fourth sefira, called *Hesed* (the language of insemination and birthing comes from the Kabbalists themselves). To put it another way, within Binah, the forces of the light begin to differentiate, and the lower sefirot emerge. This is *heh*, the world of creation. As Hesed emerges from Binah, the flow passes through another change and becomes *vav*, the energy of formation. All the ingredients are measured and mixed, and now comes the process of giving them shape. At the end of the stage of formation, we have the world of manifestation, represented by the last *heh*.

All four worlds exist in parallel to each other. All four are essential for the continuous process of Creation, and we live in all four of them simultaneously. They surround us, and yet we are usually unaware of the energy from the worlds of emanation, creation, and formation that create and sustain us. It is similar to the many other forces and phenomena around us—electrical and magnetic waves, for instance—that we cannot directly sense. We know they are active because we see the results of their movement: the light turns on in our bedroom, the radio broadcasts the music of Bach and Madonna, the microwave heats the soup. But we cannot see the energy in action.

In the same way, these three other worlds exist around us, and we constantly receive energy from them. However, unless we focus our attention on them, we are not aware of them. One of the aims of Kabbalah is to teach us how to live consciously in all of these worlds and become aware of our place in the flow of Creation.

Creation, as Kabbalists understand it, is not a one-time event that occurred billions of years ago, but rather an ongoing process, an event that occurs over and over again every billionth of a billionth of a second. It is an ever-flowing source that is constantly changing and evolving as the universe itself changes and evolves.

The flow of energy that created the universe and everything in it continues to flow with every second. In fact, it is the constant flow and interaction of the sefirot, of God's energy, that sustains the universe and powers its existence. We can liken it to the theory of the Big Bang, which proposes that objects in the universe, initially propelled apart by some vast explosion in the past, are still moving away from each other. The event occurred billions of years ago, but its energy is still active today.

This means that the universe and everything in it is constantly receiving the force and energy from God, and if one day God were to close off that source, the universe—and us in it— would cease to exist. Science tells us that the constant exchange of electrons between atoms keeps molecules intact and bound together so that thousands of those molecules can form something, such as a chair. If those molecules suddenly lost their binding power, the molecules would break down and the chair would disintegrate. We would sit on it, but it would dissolve like a cube of sugar in hot water. In the same way, God's energy keeps the universe together, on both a macro and a micro level. His energy is in the planet and the stars, but it is also in the chair.

If all of this sounds like a description of particle physics, it may be. The Kabbalists, remember, do not see a contradiction between science and religion. The scientific explanation of how the world came into being is valid for them, but it is only part of the equation. As far as Kabbalists are concerned, scientists are ignoring the all-important question behind their theories, and that is, What created the matter in the first place? What force compelled it into existence? And why was it created?

Both science and religion are means to bring us closer to the truth about our universe. They both seek to answer questions about where we came from. So essentially they emanate from the same starting point—Creation—and they lead back to the same conclusion. In the end, Kabbalah says, either path you take will lead you to the same truth: that God is the beginning and the source of all things.

The Kabbalists depict the creation of the universe as a process that is very similar to the one that scientists espouse. They say that Yes, there was some singular event that occurred many years ago, but God was the catalyst for that event and there were many other "invisible" stages to Creation which preceded that event and are beyond the abilities of science to examine. These events occurred on another level of reality, an immaterial level that cannot be measured by the tools of science currently available to us. Science lags at the rate of human comprehension. Who knows what the future will reveal?

For Kabbalists, Creation is not a question of Darwin or God, but of Darwin *and* God. They see no contradiction between the two paths. As far as they are concerned, scientists and theologians are describing the same events. Scientists are describing Creation as it occurred on the material level—involving measurable energy forces and matter—and theologians are describing Creation as it occurred on the immaterial level—the source behind those energy forces and matter. It's an idea symbolized by the popular ornament that many people put on their car trunks, which depicts the symbol of Christianity, a fish, sprouting legs and bearing the name "Darwin" on its body. It's the perfect symbol for the breeding of irrational faith with rational science.

The idea that Creation is ongoing is essential to understanding that there is an ongoing link between us and God. It is not the case that billions of years ago God's presence was felt in the world, and that today we are abandoned to our own devices. If God's energy is continually flowing into the universe to sustain everything in it, including us, then this means that God's creative energy is forever flowing in and through us too. Our connection to Him is current. If we learn to see the energy flow coming down to us, in a manner of speaking, then we can climb our way back up that flow to be closer to God.

Kabbalah teaches us how to tap into that universal flow. The sefirot on the Tree of Life are the depiction of that flow of energy. They are the means to understand God and "travel" back to Him, and by becoming aware of the creative flow that sustains us and the world, we can grow closer to God.

It is said that God created and destroyed seven universes before creating the one in which we now live. Our universe, Kabbalists tell us, is based on principles of balance and harmony. In the previous universes, justice was too severe and the universes could not survive. They needed mercy and compassion to balance harsh judgment.

The understanding is not that complete worlds were created prior to ours, but that somehow, in the process of creating, certain things happened that caused Ein Sof to abort the mission. We could look at it as a series of false starts until slight alterations in the formula made the plan finally work. The implication is one of evolution on a cosmic level, of God getting the balance right.

Some Kabbalists explain it like this: When Ein Sof contracted Himself in the process of *tzimtzum,* He achieved the contraction by separating out the powers of *Din* (judgment) within Him, and concentrating it into one place. The power of this concentrated Din overwhelmed its opposite power (compassion) and pushed it out of the space. Din was not completely alone, however—there were remnants of God's other forces left behind that would be used as some of the mixing agents for Creation—but for the most part, this space was composed of Din. The space, then, represented an absence of mercy and compassion. The process of emanation that occurred next was a process of Ein Sof pouring a mixture of compassion and mercy back into the black space, thus creating a balance.

The Kabbalists theorize that God did not put enough mercy into the previous universes, and thus these universes could not survive. Judgment is imbalanced if not softened by compassion. *Yud,* the power that brings order into the chaos of the black space, represents an act of mercy, because it is helping to balance the blackness of judgment. Kabbalists consider the emanation, then, an act of love, because God showed mercy on this Creation by ensuring that it would have a chance to survive.

Why it took God seven tries before He succeeded is not completely addressed by the Kabbalists. But some Kabbalists believe the destruction of the previous universes introduced the idea of imperfection and mistakes into our world, and that of redemption. The number seven, as was mentioned earlier, is very significant in Kabbalah and points to the final redemption. Kabbalists believe that the final redemption, the return of the many to the One, will occur in the eighth phase of our current cycle of Creation (the cycle is counted from the inception of our universe, and each phase within the cycle corresponds to a certain number of years calculated by the Kabbalists). Many of them believe that we are currently in the seventh phase.

four

UNDERSTANDING GENESIS

THE BASIC RULES OF ANALYSIS

Now that we've outlined some concepts about how the Kabbalists believe Creation happened, we can turn to the Book of Genesis and see how Kabbalists derived many of their concepts from the text. Before we go into the specifics, however, we should first examine some of the ways in which Kabbalists worked on interpreting the language of the Bible to arrive at their conclusions.

Many Kabbalists of the thirteenth century arrived at their ideas in part through prophecy, which was achieved by slipping into an ecstatic state of consciousness to obtain a mystical union with the divine realm. Kabbalists would chant the names of God like mantras, while using specific breathing techniques and body movements to manipulate the flow of energy through their body and bring on a state of awareness that would allow them to receive messages from the spiritual world. There were even very detailed Kabbalist meditation manuals written about how to achieve this state. Some Kabbalists would also meditate on the words of the Bible or on specific letters, focusing their attention on the shape or sound of the letters to divine the meaning within. By blocking out the distractions of the world, silencing the chatter in their heads, and focusing their attention on one thing, Kabbalist mystics were able to tap into a level of consciousness in which they could comprehend the divine truths or concepts that otherwise eluded them.

In addition to meditation, Kabbalists used a number of more analytical methods to examine the biblical texts themselves. For example, they examined Genesis as if using a high-powered microscope. Like good detectives, they picked through every detail—descriptions of body language, variations in the manner of speech or tone of voice (God is described as whispering, speaking softly, speaking loudly, speaking angrily), changes in verb tenses—to uncover what the Torah was saying beneath the surface, while at the same time keeping in mind what they already knew about the Torah from the fifteen-hundred-year-old written and oral traditions.

The manner in which they did this was identical to the manner that traditional rabbis studied the Bible. There are a number of principles or laws that rabbis use to study and interpret the Torah, whether reading it on a literal or a mystical level. One principle regards the repeated use of specific words or actions. If the Torah mentions something more than once, or uses the same word in different situations, the rabbis believe it is intentional, usually to teach us another lesson or added dimension about something. For example, if the act of giving charity is mentioned in two different places, each occurrence is meant to impart different aspects of the subject. The first mention might describe how much someone gave to the poor (and from this the rabbis would determine the rule for what Jewish law would consider appropriate alms-giving) and the second mention might impart how often someone gave to the poor.

In addition, there are many words that would seem to be used oddly or even incorrectly in the Torah. A grammarian might go through and red-line God's use of terms that are not used in the way we normally would use them. But a closer inspection would reveal the meaning behind the word. Take, for example, the tradition of the wedding ring. The Bible doesn't say specifically that a groom has to give his bride something of value. However, the same word that is used to describe the act of marrying a woman—*taking* a wife—is also used earlier in the Torah, when Abraham purchases a cave in Hebron in which to bury his wife, Sarah. The Torah says Abraham *takes* the cave. It's an odd use of the word, especially since Abraham actually pays money for the cave—400 shekels. Therefore the rabbis concluded that if money was exchanged when the word *take* was employed in one place, it should also be exchanged when the word is employed in the same manner elsewhere. The ring, then, became symbolic of this exchange.

There are also instances in which different words are used to describe what seems to be the same thing. Take, for example, the different words the Bible uses to describe the act of Creation in Genesis. In some places it says that God *created,* while in other places it uses the words *formed* or *made.* It might seem like splitting hairs to focus on the subtle differences between the terms, but by doing this the Kabbalists reached their conclusion that each of the different terms connoted different kinds of Creation being described: Creation as it occurred on the cosmic, conceptual level and Creation as it occurred on the physical, material level. Kabbalists also examined all the different ways in which the ten names of God were used and whether or not there was an underlying pattern. They came to the conclusion that none of these names is actually the real name of God; that the Bible in fact, as mentioned earlier, never states the true name of God; and that, indeed, there is an underlying pattern to the use of these names.

A third way Kabbalists interpreted the Bible was through Gematria, which involves the substitution of numbers for letters. Each letter in Hebrew is assigned a numerical value (see chart on page 195), and Kabbalists would add the numbers in a word to get the value of the word, then compare words of equal value to discover a deeper meaning. If the Kabbalists were unsure how to interpret one word, they would look for its numerical equivalent and try to discern the meaning of the first word based on the meaning of the second.

Some people find this aspect of Kabbalah a bit flighty and think the Kabbalists were just playing pointless word games. But the Kabbalists used these methods to expand their interpretations of the language. Through such "playing" they arrived at associations and conclusions they might not otherwise have discovered.

All of this focus on specific language leads to an essential point about Kabbalah: For Kabbalists, the Bible cannot be interpreted in any language other than Hebrew. The Hebrew alphabet is sacred because, according to Jewish tradition, it is the language that came from God and it is the tool by which God created the universe. His use of it in the Bible, Kabbalists believe, is very precise. Every letter, every word has significance, and any substitution of the words means, quite literally, that something gets lost in the translation.

A CRYSTAL-CLEAR BEGINNING

We now examine some of the specific words of Genesis to see how Kabbalists discovered various meanings in those words. While every concept in Kabbalah was derived from oral and written traditions in a painstaking process that took generations of great and dedicated minds, the most we can do here is look at one example, the opening line of Genesis, to get an idea of the complexity involved in coming to these interpretations. (My thanks to Rabbi Eliahu Klein, who aided in my understanding of the many possible nuances.)

In the beginning, God created the heavens and the earth.

The opening words here seem straightforward enough. In the beginning, God created the heavens and the earth—period. It's a simple statement of fact that seems to tell us everything we need to know about the universe. Well, it seems straightforward, but when we look at the words more closely, we see that with slight variations in the translation of the original Hebrew, we can alter our entire understanding of the events of Creation without essentially changing the concept that the words express, which is that God created the heavens and the earth.

The Hebrew phrase is *Bereshit bara Elohim ve et ha shamaim ve et ha aretz.* The first thing we should note is that the very first letter of the Bible is the Hebrew letter *bet,* the second letter of the Hebrew alphabet. We might wonder why the Bible would start its narrative with the second letter of the alphabet rather than the first. If in the beginning phrase we're talking about the beginning of Creation, why not make the form match the content and simply begin the Bible with the beginning of the alphabet?

Kabbalists say that the use of the letter *bet* shows us that something else existed before the beginning of which the Bible is speaking. Prior to "In the beginning" was God, who preceded everything, including the chaos out of which Creation grew. We understand, then, that the missing letter *aleph,* the first letter of the Hebrew alphabet that should rightly begin the book of Genesis, is not here because it represents what preceded Creation, what preceded the Book of Genesis. *Aleph* is the hidden God (Ein Sof) from which this entire story flows, and *bet* is the revealed God (the sefirot), the story of Creation itself.

Note also that the letter *aleph* is assigned the numerical value of 1 in Hebrew numerology, and the letter *bet* is assigned the value of 2. One represents unity and oneness and undifferentiation, which is a correct description of Ein Sof. The number two represents duality and differentiation, which is an accurate description of Creation, the point at which something emerged from the oneness to create something separate from that oneness.

Something else should be noted before we begin to analyze the sentence. The traditional manner of translating this first line omits one word, which turns out to be an important word for Kabbalists. The word *ve* ("and") appears twice in the sentence, which doesn't seem to make sense, so translators have traditionally left it out. Translated correctly, the sentence would read: "In the beginning, God created and the heavens and the earth." We'll discuss the significance of this later.

Let's begin, then, with the first word in the sentence, *Be,* which is attached as a prefix to the word *reshit. Be* can mean, among other things, "in," "with," or "by means of" in Hebrew, depending on the context; and the word *reshit,* which usually means "beginning," comes from the root of the word *head* and can also mean "wisdom." Therefore, if we substitute the alternative meanings, we could translate the first word as:

In the beginning. . .

With the beginning. . .

By means of the beginning. . .

In the head. . .

With the head. . .

By means of the head. . .

In wisdom. . .

With wisdom. . .

By means of wisdom. . .

Progressing to the second word in the sentence, *bara* ("created"), we find a strange conjunction with the word following it, *Elohim* (one of the Bible's names for God), which seems to suggest that the subject of the sentence is falling after the verb. Normally, however, we would put the actor before the verb: *Elohim bara*—God created. As it is, *Elohim* becomes the object of creation, and the subject of the sentence is understood as the third-person singular of the verb *bara* ("It"), which implies God. Therefore, the first part of the line reads, "In the beginning, God created God. . . ." But how can this be if God is the source of all things and has no creator?

We have to refer back to our discussion of the ten names of God to see that Elohim is only one manifestation of God.

Elohim is the name that refers to the sefira Binah, the last stage of oneness that contains the seven lower sefirot within, but it also refers to all of the sefirot collectively. When we read it this way, we understand that Ein Sof created or emanated the qualities of Himself—the sefirot—to act as agents of Creation. Thus, we have:

> In the beginning, Ein Sof created the sefirot. . .

Going back to the sentence, *Bereshit bara Elohim ve et ha shamaim ve et ha aretz,* we now arrive at the phantom *and* that we noted earlier and which now makes much more sense. God created not only the sefirot, but something else as well.

We look to the next word, *et,* to give us a clue. *Et* is generally used as a formal function word before a direct object, which is how most translators have traditionally interpreted it here. But the word *et* is also composed of the Hebrew letters *aleph* and *tav,* the first and last letters of the Hebrew alphabet. It would seem, then, that *et* is shorthand for the entire Hebrew alphabet, and if this is the case, then the translation reads:

> In the beginning, Ein Sof created the sefirot and the alphabet
> of the heaven (*ha shamaim*) and the alphabet of the earth (*ha
> aretz*).

This is a correct description of what Kabbalists say occurred. Ein Sof created the sefirot, and through them He created everything in the heavens and on the earth, everything in the universe from *A* to *Z*. But what does "the alphabet of the heaven and earth" really mean? What do letters have to do with Creation?

One of the first legends in Judaism is that God created the world through the letters of the Hebrew alphabet. Actually it says that 974 generations before God created the heaven and the earth, He created the Torah, and through the Torah He then created the universe. Through the letters of the Torah, he created all that exists in the Torah; thus He created Creation. This is an area of Kabbalah called "letter mysticism."

But how can this be, since we know that the Torah was first dictated to Moses on Mt. Sinai? Kabbalists say this doesn't mean that the specific Torah existed 974 generations before the world, but that the divine plan was "written" in the heavens. The legend tells us it was written as black fire on white fire; it existed in the "mind" of God. How Creation progressed from mind to manifestation was, at least in part, accomplished through language.

As already mentioned, when Ein Sof emanated His energy into the black space, He sent it out on the power of the letter *yud,* and it was the four letters of God's sacred name that "propelled" the energy through the four levels of Creation. The sefirot and the alphabet together gave birth to Creation. We can see this principle represented on the Tree of Life in the form of the twenty-two paths that connect the ten sefirot to each other. There are twenty-two letters in the Hebrew alphabet, and each one corresponds to a path on the Tree. Each letter of the alphabet delineates a different path the energy takes from one sefira to another. Everything in the physical world comes into being through the interconnection of these twenty-two letters and the ten sefirot. But if you look at the Tree, the paths of the letters don't just join the spheres together, they seem to be the framework for the entire structure that binds it. The Tree could easily be a molecular model depicting the binding forces of matter.

Language and speech are in fact fundamental to Creation in Genesis ("God said, 'Let there be light,' and there was light"). Every time God speaks in this first chapter of Genesis, something happens; either the waters divide, or the sun appears, or the skies fill with birds of every kind. The world is said to have been created through ten sayings. Indeed, there are ten instances in Genesis in which the words "And God said" are used, and each expression is followed by the creation of something else in the universe. These ten statements created the world.

We might dismiss the idea of letters and language being instruments of Creation as the mere mythology of an unsophisticated people, but when we look at it more closely, we see that the idea is actually very sophisticated. Remember, the Torah is a history of the universe up to and beyond the life of Moses. It preexists events and even foretells them. It appears that, in some way, by saying it is so, it becomes so; by writing it down, the words create the thing itself. (So let it be written, so let it be done.)

The idea of letters and speech having the power to conjure certain things is familiar. Speech is a tool of creation. We all

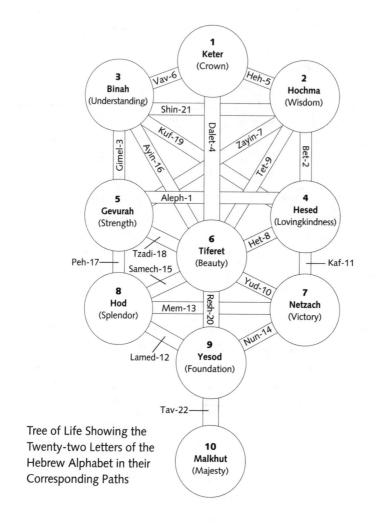

Tree of Life Showing the
Twenty-two Letters of the
Hebrew Alphabet in their
Corresponding Paths

know the power of words; once they are thrown into the world they initiate action; people interpret the words and act on them or react to them. Words set action in motion.

The alphabet can also be seen as a tool of creation because it helps put ideas or thoughts into words, it helps clothe ideas and lead them to expression, making them real. This suggests that the Hebrew alphabet was the tool for carrying the idea of Creation into being. But Kabbalists go beyond this by saying that letters and words actually create.

Linguists and philosophers have long wrestled with the idea that a word cannot be the created thing itself, but only a representation of that thing. According to Kabbalists, this is not the case with Hebrew. The word is the thing; the essence of the thing is tied to its name. This means that the word *table*, in Hebrew, *shulchan*, is closely tied to the object table, and that if the object were called something else, then it would also be something else and would no longer be a table. Something in the order of the letters that shape the word *shulchan* is the formula that creates the thing we know as a table. Alter the letters a little, create a different word, and you create a different object altogether. The Hebrew alphabet is seen by Kabbalists as a kind of code in which words are formulas for the things they express. In other words, the combination of different letters like *m-a-y-i-m* is a formula for water itself. Each letter represents a different energy or force that, when combined, create the thing the word expresses. This idea is also found in science, in which the elemental tables show how many things in the world can be reduced to a formula. Water, for instance, can be reduced to the elements of hydrogen and oxygen. Kabbalists are suggesting that in a similar way the Hebrew word for water, *mayim,* contains within it the recipe for making water. The combination of the elements represented by the Hebrew letters *m-a-y-i-m* can be used to conjure the forces that mix the elements of hydrogen and oxygen to create water. Everything that can be named can be broken down to a similar formula.

We can see the idea even more clearly when we remember that every Hebrew letter has a numerical equivalent. Take the word for water. If we say that the letters that comprise the word *mayim* represent the forces and elements that create water, we're saying also that the numerical equivalent does the same thing. We're living in an age in which genetic marking and genetic coding, which can reduce every one of us to a combination of elements and numbers, has made this much more plausible today than it must have been for the medieval Kabbalists.

We mentioned earlier that the Kabbalists kept many of their teachings secret and were selective in choosing disciples; this is one of the reasons for their secrecy. They believed that knowledge of these codes and the meditative practices that went with them could conceivably give someone the power to alter the forces of Creation. Indeed, some Kabbalists believe that this is partly what was going on when Moses divided the waters of the Red Sea.

Returning to Genesis, from the interpretation of this one line we can see how careful analysis and subtle changes in translation can lead to entirely different descriptions of what happened. This one little phrase contains 1) the basic idea that God created the heavens and the earth; 2) the idea that letters and speech are tools for creation (on a basic and mystical level); and 3) the idea that words and numbers form the basic formulas for all things in the universe. This one line contains a scenario of Creation that speaks to spiritualists, to linguists and philosophers, and to mathematicians and scientists. We've taken different paths but have arrived at the same thing. Just like the paths on the Tree of Life, which all start from the same place—God—and end in the same place—Creation of the heavens and the earth. This gives us one idea of the breadth and scope that Kabbalah encompasses, and helps to explain why Kabbalah can be a lifelong intellectual pursuit. Convoluted as it seems, however, Kabbalah can also be immensely beautiful.

Moving along then, this first line of Genesis, Kabbalists believe, is followed by a description of how the stage was set for Creation—the contraction of God ("The earth was without form and void, with darkness over the face of the abyss") and the emanation ("God's spirit moved on the water's surface"). Then the rest of the chapter runs through the days of Creation.

Kabbalists believe, however, that this is not a description of physical Creation, but a description of Creation on the cosmic, macro level. The opening lines of Genesis aren't describing the actual physical creation of the birds and the bees and the flowers and the trees. They're describing the cosmic prelude—the *tzimtzum* and the emanation of all the forces of Creation that will then be responsible for creating the birds and the bees. Each day of Creation that follows describes a sefira coming into being. Each day describes another of God's qualities concentrating itself into a vessel. It isn't until chapters 2 and 3 of Genesis that Kabbalists believe physical Creation is actually being addressed. Going back to the first line of Genesis, then, if we substitute the words "In the head" for "In the beginning," we can see that it suggests that this Creation is taking place on a non-material level. It's all in God's head.

How else do we know that this is not referring to the real Creation? Because in chapter 1 of Genesis we have one account of Creation and in chapter 2, we have a second account using different words to describe the same things. However, the name for God changes in chapter 2 and the word "created" in chapter 1 becomes "formed" in chapter 2. We've moved from the world of Briyah (creation) to the world of Yetzirah (formation). Kabbalists, by the way, do not end chapter 1 with the Creation of humans on the sixth day as do most translated Bibles; instead, they end it on the seventh day after the words: "And God blessed the seventh day and declared it holy, because it was the day when he ceased this work of creation." Chapter 2 then begins with, "Here is a summary of the events in the creation of the heavens and earth. . . ."

Why do we need a summary of everything that's just been summarized—particularly when that summary is nearly as long as the original? One phrase that depicts an essential Kabbalistic thought is, "As above, so below." It expresses the idea that everything that happens in the physical realm has a model in the spiritual realm; everything that happens in our world has a precedent in the higher world. The process of Creation in the spiritual world—that is, the creation of the sefirot as discussed in chapter 1—is a model for what happens all over again on the next level. This is why in the second chapter of Genesis, God begins His story all over again.

Again, we learn about the birds and the bees and the flowers and the trees. God the Gardener is planting humans' little island of paradise, giving it all sorts of beautiful vegetation and digging a system of four tributaries through which the river waters of Eden can flow and nourish it. At the center of the garden He plants two trees: the Tree of Life and the Tree of Knowledge.

But this time the Bible gives us details about how human beings were created. It tells us that God formed Adam's body from the soil of the earth (the name *Adam* comes from the Hebrew word for earth or soil, *adamah,* and the word for blood, *dam*; thus Adam was made flesh and blood). And when the body is finished, God breathes into the body "the breath of life." The Hebrew word for breath is *neshima,* which shares the same root as the Hebrew word for soul, *neshama.*

If this refers to our soul, then we're still not in the physical world, the world of manifestation, the word of Assiyah. If the *tzimtzum* and the emanation are the first world (Atzilut), and the creation of the sefirot from Binah are the second world (Briyah), we are now in the world of formation (Yetzirah). If we look closely, we can see a description of the *tzimtzum* and emanation all over again. The chapter begins with a description of the earth that God created. It tells us that the earth is barren, with neither plant nor grain sprouting from it, due to the fact that God hasn't sent any rain. (It is desolate, similar to the space of nothingness created by the *tzimtzum.*) God then breathes into Man (compare with the emanation) and begins to plant the garden (inseminates Binah). In the middle of the Garden, He places the Tree of Life (*Tiferet,* the symbol of harmony and balance) as well as the Tree of Knowledge (an eleventh sefira is sometimes placed on the Kabbalah Tree, and is called *Da'at*—Hebrew for knowledge). Then He digs the four rivers (the four sefirot that stand on either side of Tiferet), and finally he places Adam in the garden (*Yesod,* the foundation sefira). But what about *Malkhut,* the last sefira on the Tree? That's where the story of the Fall comes in.

It's significant that the primary symbol of Kabbalah is called the Tree of Life. Indeed, Kabbalists believe that the Tree of Life mentioned in Genesis is actually a reference to the sefirot, which were fully in place once the "creation" stage of Creation was complete; that is, once Creation had passed from the world of Briyah (creation) in chapter 1 to the world of Yetzirah (formation) in chapter 2.

Unlike with the Tree of Knowledge, Adam and Eve were originally permitted to eat from the Tree of Life; they had free access to its fruits. This means they were connected directly to the universal flow of energy through the sefirot and could commune easily with God whenever they wanted. But once Adam and Eve tasted fruit from the Tree of Knowledge, they were also prohibited from eating from the Tree of Life, and indeed were ultimately banished from the Garden altogether. How do we interpret this?

It's only after Adam and Eve eat the fruit from the Tree of Knowledge that they become aware that they are naked and experience shame. It's a symbol of the final step in Creation, of the final physical manifestation of the forces of God. Prior to the Fall, Adam and Eve exist in the world of Yetzirah, the world of the spirit. After the Fall, however, the souls that are Adam and Eve become clothed in physical form and they become aware of their nakedness. A line in chapter 3 says that after the sin, God made "garments of skin" to clothe Adam and Eve. Until the Fall, they are souls in the world of Yetzirah; after the Fall, they descend to the world of Assiyah (physical manifestation).

So what is this story all about? What is the meaning of Creation, and what is the meaning of Adam and Eve's sin?

In the literal interpretation of Adam and Eve, we have two historical figures, two distinct individuals who are depicted as the first ancestors of all humankind. But Kabbalists, rather than viewing Adam and Eve as historical figures, view them as archetypal symbols of the splitting of oneness that initiated Creation in the first place. We've all heard the idea that man and woman complete each other; it's a familiar concept that has wound its way into popular romance—the idea of finding a soulmate. Kabbalists believe that the story of Adam and Eve is an allegory for how the concept of duality became actualized in our world, and how the entire aim of Creation is to rejoin the parts into the one. Here's how it works:

Jewish tradition holds that originally Adam and Eve were not created as two separate beings but started out as a single entity with two faces. We see the basis for this in Genesis 1:27 when it says that on the sixth day of Creation, "Like God did God make man; Man and maid did he make them." Here we have God making both man and woman, and yet we don't have the creation of Eve from Adam's rib until much later in Genesis 2:22. Therefore, we understand that what God created at this stage was a united being, within which existed the dualities of male and female. Actually, to be precise about it, the being contained all the dualities and qualities of all the sefirot. How do we know this? From the line preceding the one just quoted. "Then God said, 'Let us make Man in our image.'" Note the plurals *us* and *our*. The name for God used here in the Bible is Elohim, which, as we noted earlier, represents all of the sefirot together. Thus we understand that it is not God making the statement, but the sefirot. It is the forces of God speaking, and they are talking about creating human beings in their image, in the image of the sefirot. They are modeling human beings on the ten qualities of God that are the forces of Creation. This is what we mean when we say that the Tree of Life and the sefirot are a model of humans.

At this stage in chapter 1, the stage of Briyah (creation), the being called Adam contains the dualities of masculine and feminine united as one. But they cannot look at each other. The legend tells us that the two faces are turned away from each other and cannot see each other. So God, in chapter 2, performs an operation, separating the single entity into two. The Hebrew says not that God took Eve from Adam's rib, but that He took her from his side, meaning that they were joined together like Siamese twins. He creates two halves so that each can turn to look at the other. In doing so, he creates the duality of humans. But remember, this is still on the spiritual level. We're still in the world of Yetzirah in chapter 2, before the Fall initiates the world of manifestation.

The idea that Adam and Eve are separated so that they can turn to look at each other is an example of the philosophical concept of the Other. In order to know that I exist, I need the

Other outside me to define me. I exist as me because I am not you. Otherwise, without you, without something outside me, I am the whole world. Freud theorized that the infant recognizes herself and begins to establish her identity only when she recognizes that her mother is something apart from herself. She begins to understand who she is by understanding who she is not. Prior to this, she thinks the entire world, including her mother, is an extension of herself. Only when she "turns to face" her mother, does the child see that her mother is outside of herself, and she begins to develop her own sense of identity. Thus the act of Adam and Eve looking at each other, the act of the two halves turning to face each other, is the recognition of identity and difference.

But the Fall also represents one of the ways in which we arrive at knowledge. Often we can't know what something is without comparing it to something else. Once Adam and Eve eat the fruit of Knowledge, they not only see that there is a difference between good and evil, but also understand what that difference is. Knowledge and understanding represent the beginning of differentiation. It's the difference between simply seeing two things—good and evil—and knowing the difference between them. Good and evil existed before Adam and Eve ate from the Tree, but there was nothing to distinguish them from each other. It is interesting to note that Adam gives Eve her name only after the Fall, recognizing that she is truly different from him. Actually, he comes to know her better than we can imagine, because the next chapter begins with the statement, "And so Adam knew Eve his wife."

Of course we're talking here about knowledge "in the Biblical sense."

WHY CREATION?

We've examined the texts of Genesis to see how Creation is depicted, and we've listed several principles to see how Kabbalists believe it was accomplished. But why did it occur in the first place?

It's one of the trickier areas of Kabbalah, because any theory about why God did this or that suggests that we can know what was on God's mind or even that God has a mind.

The burning question is, Why did God create the universe? Why did He break away from Himself and go from the one to the many? According to Kabbalists, God created in order to "know" Himself. As we said about the infant, in order for her to fully recognize her identity there has to be someone outside herself. It's a little like that Zen koan about the sound of one hand clapping. There is no relationship, and no realization of the self, without another. So God sent a part of Himself outside Himself in order to undergo a process of evolution and return to Himself a higher being, a being that knows Himself.

All of this is a complex way of saying that God creates in order to know His own goodness; and He creates the duality of good and evil in order to recognize the difference between them. Before Creation, God is a king without a kingdom. He's a giver without anyone to receive. The only problem is that in the process of creating life He also creates a problem.

Creation was initially an act of love that went wrong due to human free will. Kabbalists say that Adam and Eve were originally supposed to stay in the Garden of Eden, to exist as spiritual beings, but they departed from the plan, and as a result the balance was broken; the free flow of energy from above to below and back again was thwarted. Adam and Eve introduced new elements into the equation. Or did they? After all, God is omniscient and He must have known what they would do.

While the consequence of the sin of Adam and Eve is a regretful one (there are no rewards or punishment in Kabbalah, only consequences), it is perhaps a necessary one. Unlike the traditional reading of the Bible, which places blame on Adam and Eve and straps us all with original sin before we're born, Kabbalists believe the soul needed to descend in order for it to evolve. The "punishment" was actually an act of love designed to elevate souls from a point of simple knowledge to conscious understanding (it's not just that I know; it's that *I know* I know). The aim is for all the many parts of God to return to the oneness, but to an even more powerful oneness than existed before. "Know thyself" seems to be the axiom of Creation, and to know thyself means to know all the parts of thyself. But sometimes we need to step outside of ourselves in order to have the best perception, and this seems to be what God did through the act of Creation: He stepped outside Himself.

REDEMPTION IN KABBALAH

Jewish legend tells how, when God was preparing to make the world and told the Torah of His plans for human beings, the Torah complained that humans would be sinful and wouldn't follow the laws that God had written for them. God replied, "Repentance was created by Me long ago, and people who are sinful will be able to mend their ways and be forgiven by Me."

The whole idea of repentance is important to Creation, because those who plummet to the depths of darkness are said to stand more brightly in the light than those who never leave it. The repenter is stronger than the person who is always righteous, because the repenter has had farther to climb back. He's had to battle impulses and overcome them, while the righteous has not even exercised a muscle. The Bible hints at many ideas of second chances. There are many instances of the second-born child being chosen over the first-born. Moses was the second-born son, as was Jacob. In addition, the Ten Commandments were destroyed by God when he discovered the Israelites' golden calf, but Moses convinced Him to create a second set.

Sin and redemption are necessary to the goal of knowing ourselves. To be good without knowledge of bad, Kabbalists believe, is not real goodness. This does not mean, however, that

Kabbalists are advocating that we act badly so that we can then repent. It means simply that we have to recognize the dark sides of ourselves first, acknowledge their existence in us, before we can truly know both sides and then turn from the dark to the light. To have faced the depths of darkness within us gives us more appreciation for the light. On an individual psychological level this seems to be good medicine for the psyche as well, since it's known that the more we deny or repress aspects of ourselves the more they insist on asserting themselves.

The Kabbalists are suggesting that the path to wholeness and balance is to accept that we contain many aspects, none of which is bad or harmful unless it is out of balance. The existence of evil is also important, because choice is essential if goodness is to mean anything. If we do what we are told, it doesn't have the same meaning as if we do something because we choose to do it. But in order to turn away from something, we have to first acknowledge its existence; we have to identify the darkness in ourselves in order to turn away from it.

This lesson is repeated in the upper world where, in the course of Creation, God created darkness into which He then poured His light. This leads Kabbalists to the understanding that there can be no darkness without light. We define darkness as the absence of light. Some modern Kabbalists have likened it to the Chinese yin and yang symbol. You can't draw the symbol for yin without also drawing the symbol for yang. In order to appreciate the light, to know the light, we need to see the darkness. We need to find the light in the darkness in order to bring the light out of it—what is a black hole but a place where light is trapped?

"As above, so below," thus, suggests that the entire scenario of the Fall was a setup, and that a model for repentance was already engraved in the divine plan. We already saw one example of repentance with the destruction of the previous worlds. God made a mistake and had to right it. But Kabbalists say a second event occurred during the creation of the sefirot that also set a precedent for reparation. When the sefirot were initially formed, God poured too much energy into them and the vessels shattered, sending sparks of energy flying; the vessels couldn't contain Him. Kabbalists call this "the breaking of the vessels," vessels referring to the sefirot once they were in place to receive Ein Sof's energy. The sefirot were not destroyed completely, but were full of cracks, and God had to repair them. The light was then reduced and the project resumed. This set a precedent for repentance. But reparation is not complete; when God fixed the vessels, it is said, Malkhut, the last sefira, remained cracked, and it is our job to repair it. In the world of Yetzirah, Adam's Fall repeated the breaking of the vessels.

TIKKUN HA OLAM

Isaac Luria divides Creation into three realms: the *tzimtzum;* the breaking of the vessels; and the *tikkun* (repair). One of the most important concepts in Kabbalah involves the final reparation and healing of the world (*tikkun ha olam*), which has to be completed by humans.

According to Kabbalists, Creation was a process of exile, of God exiling Himself. When God contracted Himself in the *tzimtzum,* He removed Himself from Himself, then sent a part of Himself into the darkness to create our world. Malkhut, the end result of that process of Creation, is the symbol of exile. God sent the sefirot out of Him into that removed space to create the world, and as a result, Kabbalists say God sent part of Himself into exile. Exile is not a happy experience. The Israelites lived in exile in Babylonia for forty-seven years, and were, after the destruction of the Second Temple, exiled for another 1,878 years. The exile of God means that God is not whole in some way. Something is divided from God that was formerly united with Him. There is a division in Him, and thus a rift in harmony.

The theme of exile is repeated on each level of Creation. On the second day of Creation, it is described how God divided the vapors "to form the sky above and the oceans below." He divided them horizontally. The Kabbalists see this as the beginning of the division of the spiritual and physical worlds that, until then, were one. Then the parting continues with the division of the single human being into two, Adam and Eve. And finally comes the last separation with the banishment of Adam and Eve from the Garden of Eden.

According to Gershom Scholem, the original "sin" was the separation of the spiritual and physical, where before there was unity. Every sin thereafter, he says, is a mimic of this separation, a mimic of the act of getting farther from God, of the exile from God. Part of the repair work that we have to do, then, is to rejoin the physical and spiritual, to elevate the physical world to its former place of union with the spiritual. The aim of Kabbalah is to teach us how to reconnect the two: how to elevate the physical to the spiritual. Understand, though, that this does not mean that the physical world is inferior. Just because it sits on the bottom rung of the Creation ladder does not make it less important than the top. The physical world is, in fact, essential to evolution because it is only in this world that final reparation and evolution can be accomplished, because it is only in this world that division has been made real. It is through our experiences in the physical world that we bring about repair in the spiritual. Evolution could not occur in the spiritual realm alone. It requires lessons that can only be learned in the physical world.

Repentance is essential to the repair of the world and the return to wholeness. The Hebrew word for repentance, *teshuva,* also means "return." A return from where we came, which is central to the Kabbalist idea of healing the universe and returning to unity.

Humans alone, of all the creatures God created, have free will. In this we are Godlike. We are not mindless followers of God; we are also creators like God and our actions have the ability to affect and alter Creation. The story of Adam and Eve teaches us that we have a crucial role in Creation. In the idyllic Eden, God gave Adam the role of naming the things in the Garden. This means that God gave us a role in Creation, and not an insignificant role at that, since naming the thing is like dotting the *i* and crossing the *t* of Creation. After God created the light in chapter 1 of Genesis, He named the light "day" and the dark "night." The naming of the thing completes the process of its creation. The fact that God lets Adam name the beings in the Garden reveals, for Kabbalists, that God gives us the role of completing the Creation process. It wasn't until the last moments before sundown on the last day of Creation that God finally got around to making a human being. This could either mean that humans were so insignificant that we were the last thing God made; or more likely, that we were the crowning glory of Creation. The entire stage was set for our entrance.

It is said that the letters of the Tetragrammaton, the letters that represent the four worlds of Creation, are not united for as long as we are in exile from God; this is why the name YHWH is not spoken. Only when redemption occurs, when all the worlds are one again, will the name of God be pronounced. Will this ever happen? Evolution of the worlds, by definition, moves forward, not backward. Each world, Kabbalists say, is evolving toward *tikkun*. Although we may take steps backward in order to do so—like God removing Himself—the eventual propulsion is always forward.

five

THE TREE OF LIFE

THE SYSTEM

The Tree of Life is the main symbol of Kabbalah and represents the essence of a belief system that can only be described in symbolism. It is essentially a map depicting the ongoing events and forces of Creation as they are described in Genesis. It is the Kabbalists' attempt at visualizing forces that we cannot see. We cannot see Creation itself, but we can see the results of the process of Creation.

In addition to being a map of Creation, the Tree is also the place where we begin to see how Kabbalah relates to us on the human level by showing us our place in the universe and our role in the flow of energy that sustains all things and all life within it.

As we already know, the Tree of Life is composed of ten vessels, depicted as circles (the sefirot) on the Tree, and twenty-two connecting paths that run horizontally, vertically, and diagonally between them. These are the varied paths that the energy of Ein Sof follows. The sefirot and the numbered paths are the engines behind the laws of the universe, the laws of nature. These paths plus the ten sefirot equal thirty-two, which Kabbalists call the wondrous paths of wisdom.

As mentioned before, each path represents a letter of the Hebrew alphabet, which are partners with the sefirot in Creation, and each sefira represents a stage of Creation as depicted in Genesis. For instance, each day in Genesis is characterized by a different act of Creation. On one day God creates light, on another day He creates celestial bodies—the sun, moon, and stars—and on another day He creates flora and fauna. According to Kabbalists, each of these acts, each step in Creation, signifies a different sefira coming into play. But there are ten sefirot and only seven days in Creation. This is because the top three sefirot—*Keter, Hochma,* and *Binah*—represent "hidden" stages of Creation that occurred prior to the first day described in Genesis: that is, they refer to the *tzimtzum,* the emanation of the Ein Sof Or, and the emergence of duality at the "tip" of the Ein Sof Or. These events are described in the first and second verses of Genesis, which we examined in chapter 4, that set the scene for what unfolds over seven days. The first day of Creation, then, actually corresponds to the fourth sefira on the Tree (*Hesed* or Lovingkindness). "Then God said, 'Let there be light.' And light appeared. And God was pleased with it, and divided the light from the darkness."

The second day corresponds with *Gevurah* (Strength). "Let the vapors [waters] separate to form the sky above and the oceans below."

The third day corresponds with *Tiferet* (Beauty). "Let the earth burst forth with every sort of grass and seed-bearing plant. . . ."

The fourth day corresponds with *Netzach* (Victory). "Let there be bright lights in the sky to give light to the earth. . . . They shall bring about the seasons on the earth, and mark the days and years."

The fifth day corresponds with *Hod* (Splendor). "Let the waters teem with fish and other life and let the skies be filled with birds of every kind."

The sixth day corresponds with *Yesod* (Foundation). This is the day on which human beings were created. "Then God said, 'Let us make a man—someone like ourselves.'"

The seventh day, the last day of Creation in which no activity occurs, corresponds with *Malkhut* (Majesty). The seventh day is the Sabbath, the day of rest (coming from the Hebrew word *shavat* for "rest"), which represents the finalization of Creation, or at least the finalization of this initial cycle of Creation, since we know that Creation is continuous. Every other sefira contains within it a quality that performs a function; but Malkhut is not active in the same way that the other sefirot are. Instead, it is the result of the work of the others and is the recipient of the energy

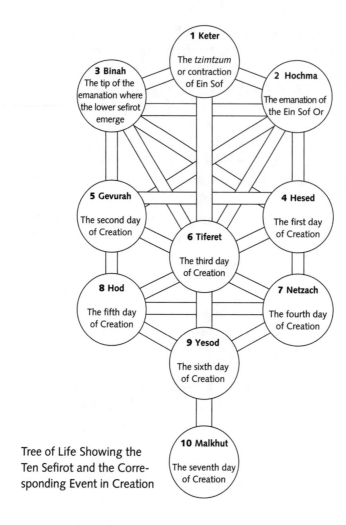

1 Keter

The *tzimtzum* or contraction of Ein Sof

3 Binah

The tip of the emanation where the lower sefirot emerge

2 Hochma

The emanation of the Ein Sof Or

5 Gevurah

The second day of Creation

4 Hesed

The first day of Creation

6 Tiferet

The third day of Creation

8 Hod

The fifth day of Creation

7 Netzach

The fourth day of Creation

9 Yesod

The sixth day of Creation

10 Malkhut

The seventh day of Creation

Tree of Life Showing the Ten Sefirot and the Corresponding Event in Creation that flows down through them. Malkhut is viewed as the sum total of the work of all the sefirot, just as the Sabbath is the sum total of the week.

The sefirot are laid out in the order in which Creation unfolded: 1) Keter; 2) Hochma; 3) Binah; 4) Hesed; 5) Gevurah; 6) Tiferet; 7) Netzach; 8) Hod; 9) Yesod; and 10) Malkhut. Visually, the sefirot are depicted on the Tree as three vertically stacked triangles, with Malkhut below them at the bottom. In other words, the top three (Keter, Hochma, Binah) form the top triangle; the next three (Hesed, Gevurah, and Tiferet) form the middle triangle; and the three after that (Netzach, Hod, and Yesod) form the bottom triangle. The top triangle is usually separated slightly from the lower ones, because the three sefirot in it represent the hidden part of Creation, a realm that is beyond our capacity to know (sometimes they are depicted behind a veil), whereas the lower seven represent the realm of the revealed and are more accessible to us.

Ten, like the number seven, is a significant figure in the Bible—there are ten plagues on Egypt and Ten Commandments, for example. In the wider universe, however, ten represents the primordial numbers zero through nine, from which all other numbers are composed. The parallel, of course, is that the ten sefirot represent the forces from which everything in the universe is created.

The reason the sefirot are laid out in triangles is because they tend to work in relationships of three. In the top triangle, Keter

132

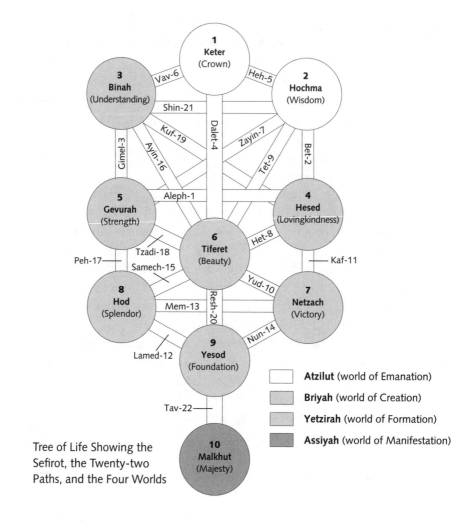

Tree of Life Showing the
Sefirot, the Twenty-two
Paths, and the Four Worlds

and Hochma produce Binah. In the two lower triangles, the middle sefira is the balancing or harmonizing point for the two sefirot on either side of it. Therefore, Tiferet (Beauty) is the balance between the forces of Hesed (Lovingkindness) and Gevurah (Strength); and Yesod (Foundation) is the balance between the forces of Hod (Splendor) and Netzach (Victory). The sefirot on the lower two triangles represent the relationship between opposing forces and a balancing force that is composed of the two opposing forces. Furthermore, the sefirot on the right side are referred to as masculine, the sefirot on the left side as feminine. The center sefirot are a combination of the two sides and therefore contain both masculine and feminine within them. Do not mistake, as many people do, that these labels designate masculine and feminine traits as we know them. The Kabbalists refer to masculine and feminine sefirot simply to illustrate opposing forces. They do not define masculine as something aggressive in the way that we might, and feminine as nurturing; they define them by sefirot that are givers (in sexual terms the man delivers the seed) and sefirot that are receptors (the woman receives the seed). Indeed, it can be confusing to understand the sefirot in terms of traditional beliefs about masculine and feminine because Kabbalists place Gevurah (Strength) on the feminine side, and Hesed (Lovingkindness) on the masculine side. The designation of masculine and feminine can be further misleading because all the sefirot contain masculine and feminine traits in them; all essentially give and receive as the energy of

Ein Sof flows down the Tree and through them. All the sefirot together unite the male and female aspects of God. This duality of masculine and feminine is evident even in the God name Elohim that stands for all of the sefirot together. The word *Elohim*, Kabbalists point out, is composed of a feminine singular root with a masculine plural ending, *im*.

If the Tree is a map of everything in the universe, then it is also, most significantly, a map of us. As we said earlier, the sefirot created human beings in "their" image; therefore, everything that human beings are composed of—every organ and every body part on an organic level, and every thought and emotion on an inorganic level—existed in the Tree first. Human beings have four elemental parts to them—the spiritual, the intellectual, the emotional, and the physical—and each of these is represented by one of the four worlds that Kabbalists say compose our universe. The first world (Atzilut) represents our spiritual nature; the second world (Briyah) represents our intellectual nature; the third world (Yetzirah) represents our emotional nature; and the fourth world (Assiyah) represents our physical nature. What this means is that if we look at the characteristics of the sefirot in each world and the qualities they manifest, we can begin to understand something about our own nature that corresponds to each sefira. For instance, Keter, in the world of Atzilut that is closest to Ein Sof, represents our individual soul's connection to the universal soul that joins us all. Binah, which deals with knowledge and understanding, represents our intellectual nature or the side of us that attempts to make sense of the world and aid in our awareness of it. The next six sefirot deal with how we process the world and how we act according to the emotions that this processing produces. Finally, Malkhut, in the world of Assiyah, represents our physical nature—such as our five senses, our passions for food, sex, beautiful art.

Following is a list of the sefirot, broken into these four elemental categories, along with a description of some of the characteristics that Kabbalists say are found in each sefira. In chapter 6, we will address in greater detail how each of these characteristics relates to human beings and their nature; for now, however, we'll focus on where each sefira fits into the process of Creation, with a brief note about its relevance to human nature. Keep in mind that over the years different Kabbalists have developed different interpretations of what each sefira represents, so there is no definitive interpretation of the Tree. But the following descriptions offer a general breakdown of the characteristics of the Tree.

THE SEFIROT

The Spiritual
(Atzilut—World of Emanation)

1 Keter, whose English name is "crown," is the first sefira and represents the unfathomable divine will in the Creation process. It is the will before there is thought or idea. It is the *tzimtzum,* the contraction of Ein Sof, that is created at the moment that the idea of Creation emerges in Ein Sof. Keter is assigned the number 1, because it represents singleness and unity. It's the most ephemeral of the sefirot and the least understood because it is the highest up on the ladder of Creation and the closest to Ein Sof. Above Keter is the realm of infinity, which we cannot comprehend with our limited human understanding. While Keter may be closest to the source, Kabbalists say that a vast abyss still separates it from Ein Sof. It is there and yet far from being there. It is sometimes referred to as nothingness—that is, No-Thing-ness—because, like Ein Sof, it is undifferentiated. Kabbalists do not delve too deeply into the nature of Keter, because it is in a realm beyond our understanding. On the human level, however, Keter represents selflessness and the obliteration of the ego, as it is here where unity of all exists and there are no individuals.

2 Hochma is called "wisdom" in English and is the second sefira, which represents the emanation into the *tzimtzum* in the process of Creation. It represents pure, undifferentiated thought. It is the thought of Creation that comes out of the will to create. It is thought emanated into the cosmos that gives form to the divine will. It is not yet a good thought or a bad thought, it is simply a thought without personality or characteristics assigned to it; it is a thought or an axiom that just is, without qualifying judgments attached to it. It is $E = mc^2$ without knowledge of what that means, or it is the thought "hunger" without an understanding of what that implies. Hochma is as-

signed the number 2 because it represents "the Other" that needs to exist before the one can be recognized. Thought exists to acknowledge and recognize the existence of the Will. Hochma on the human level represents pure, undifferentiated awareness; awareness and observation that is unmasked by judgment. It is the act of living in the moment and of simply being aware of our place in the universe.

The Intellectual

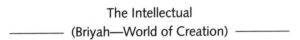 (Briyah—World of Creation)

3 Binah is called "understanding" in English and is the third sefira, which flows from Hochma. It is the point at the end of the emanation at which the lower sefirot representing duality are conceived and from which they are given birth. Binah represents the application of logic and evaluation to thoughts to make sense out of the pure thought of Hochma. It also represents differentiation, understanding the difference between one thing and another or between ourselves and "the Other." It symbolizes the beginning of duality, the understanding of the difference between good and evil, male and female. On the human level, Binah represents integration, since it is the point in which duality has not yet become differentiated. This is integration on a cosmic level—the integration of all animate and inanimate life—and on an internal level in terms of the integration of all aspects of ourselves—the masculine and feminine, the strong and the vulnerable, the intellectual and the physical.

The Emotional
——————— (Yetzirah—World of Formation) ———————

The next six sefirot together, one could say, make the world go 'round. It is the constant flux of energy among them that determines the defining characteristics of our world at any one time. For instance, if an abundance of Gevurah energy is released and is not balanced by Hesed energy, the result is a world that is harsh and constraining and full of conflict and tension from people fighting restraints that are too tight. In Kabbalah, we get the world that we create. In this sense, Kabbalists view people like Hitler and Idi Amin and events like wars and disease as the result of certain energies and actions. Nothing occurs in a vacuum. Therefore, our actions today create the world we receive tomorrow.

4 Hesed, which is called "lovingkindness" in English, is the fourth sefira and the first to emerge from Binah. Hesed, along with the next five sefirot, represent the formation stage in Creation, in which the forces of God begin to interact to bring the original will and thought to fruition. The aspect or force of God that Hesed represents is unmitigated compassion and mercy. On a human level, it represents charity, healing, nurturing, and all the other ways in which we give ourselves to the world and our compassion to other people. It is the giving of aid to refugees and victims of hurricane and flooding, or simply the giving of time to a troubled friend. All extremes have a downside, however, and the downside of unmitigated love, love that has no limits or boundaries, is obsessiveness and smothering. This is a matter of giving where giving isn't needed or wanted or in which the giving is a matter of ego and focuses more on the person doing the giving than on the person receiving. Hesed also represents the absence of borders, whether this means the absence of laws or mores in a society, the absence of parental discipline in a family, or the absence of boundaries that stop other people from walking all over us.

5 Gevurah is called "strength" and is the fifth sefira. It is the opposite of Hesed. Where Hesed is all-out giving, Gevurah represents holding back, boundaries, discipline, and limitations. It is the rules that guide and teach us and put order in society, and it is the restraint that keeps us from overindulging our passions or giving into our lazy side. The extreme side of Gevurah, when it is unbalanced by Hesed, means overly constricting boundaries and oppression. It can range from a fascist police state to an overly disciplinarian parent. It is harsh judgment and mercilessness in the absence of compassion. It is unjust suffering and the punishment of innocent victims.

6 Tiferet, the sixth sefira, is known as "beauty," not in the sense of physical beauty, but in the sense of balance and harmony. It is the balance between Hesed and Gevurah, a combination of the right amount of lovingkindness with the right amount of structure and strength. This is the balance point of giving and receiving. It is the symbol of justice with her scales equally balanced, and it is the symbol of nature in balance.

7 Netzach is known as "victory" or "triumph" and is the seventh sefira. It refers to domination and confidence, which cause harsh and overwhelming aspects when unbalanced by vulnerabilities, or giving and nurturing when paired with respect and acceptance. Netzach is sometimes compared to a parent, while its counterpart, Hod, is compared to the child. Netzach, as the dominating and confident force, nurtures and leads those who are weaker and innocent. It takes action when action is needed and assumes leadership.

8 Hod, the eighth sefira, is called "splendor" and refers to vulnerability as well as complacency and acceptance. Hod, as mentioned above, is the child to Netzach's parent. It is dependence and admiration compared to Netzach's confident independence.

9 Yesod, the ninth sefira, is known as "foundation," and is the balance between Netzach and Hod, between domination and innocence. It refers to the dynamic dance of giving and receiving, dependence and independence, and to the admiration, leadership, and respect that balance relationships between people.

The Physical
———— (Assiyah—World of Manifestation) ————

10 Malkhut is known as "majesty" or "kingdom" and refers to the physical manifestation of Ein Sof and Creation. Malkhut is the end result of the emanation from Ein Sof. It symbolizes the presence of God in our world. Malkhut is often likened to the moon, because the moon has no power or light of its own but only receives light from the sun. Malkhut is also seen as God in exile. Kabbalists call God in exile the *Shekinah,* the feminine presence of God. It is the queen exiled from her king, and exile persists for as long as the king and queen are not united. It was believed by the early Israelites that the Shekinah dwelled in the Ark in the Temple in Jerusalem. But Kabbalists believe that, in essence, we are the Shekinah. The king is represented on the Tree by Tiferet, the symbol of balance and harmony. Tiferet stands in the spiritual world while we stand in the physical one. Tiferet and Shekinah were divided with the Fall of Adam and Eve. Therefore when Kabbalists speak of the union of Tiferet and Malkhut, they're talking about a symbolic union that expresses a desire to reunite the physical and spiritual worlds.

WHAT IT SAYS ABOUT US

If the account of Creation is an account of the creation of everything in the universe, then the Tree of Life must represent everything that the universe encompasses. This means that everything in the universe must fit somewhere on the map, either in a sefira, or on one of the paths. Each sefira has, in addition to the qualities just described, a seemingly unlimited number of things that it represents. For instance, every sefira has a corresponding Jewish ancestor assigned to it (Hesed, for instance, is Abraham; Gevurah is Isaac; Netzach is Moses; Hod is Aaron). This means that each patriarch was defined by a quality that also defines that particular sefira. Moses and Aaron, for instance, were prophets, and Netzach and Hod are viewed as the forces of prophecy. Each sefira has a corresponding name of God; a Jewish holiday; a body part; a plant; an animal; a chemical element; a number; an emotion; even a color assigned to it. There are so many symbols that it can make a crowded map if you tried to include them all. But if you took a sheet of Mylar plastic, like the kind you find in anatomy books, and drew a diagram of one Tree containing just the names of God on the sefirot; then you took another sheet and wrote just the qualities of Ein Sof on the sefirot; and another one depicting the names of animals or body parts on the corresponding sefirot; . . . if you continued this for a dozen or so Mylar sheets and stacked all the sheets on top of each other, you'd have some idea of all the things the Tree encompasses.

In addition to the aspect of God that defines each sefira, each sefira also comprises all the other sefirot. Each sefira contains within it a microcosm of the entire Tree of Life. Furthermore, all sefirot are active in each world. You could represent this by drawing a vertical column of four trees on a sheet of paper, one above the other. This is why we say that everything under the sun exists in the sefirot; every emotion, feeling, or action we could possibly think of, has its parallel somewhere in the Tree. There is nothing that exists in this world that is not modeled in the Tree and the sefirot. Which means that each sefira contains all of the forces of Creation in some measure, with one defining force being the dominant one. This is similar to the way that people contain a compendium of attributes, but one defining characteristic is usually more pronounced in each person than others. Each sefira, then, has many layers within it, and each layer combines and mixes with the layers of other sefirot, creating numerous, possibly infinite combinations of new energies. It is similar, for instance, to a basic cake recipe containing flour, sugar, eggs, butter, baking powder, and milk. Slight variations in the amount of each ingredient produce a different flavored cake. Leave one ingredient out, or add another one, such as cinnamon or chocolate, and the cake takes on an entirely different flavor and texture. Such is the way with the sefirot.

Following is a chart of the sefirot listing the Hebrew name for each (along with the English translation of the name), the quality of God that defines it, the name of God in the Bible that refers to it, and the body part to which it corresponds.

─────── Table of the Sefirot ───────

Hebrew (English Name)	Quality	God Name	Body Part
1 Keter (Crown)	Enlightenment	Ehiyeh Asher Ehiyeh	Head
2 Hochma (Wisdom)	Divine Wisdom	Yah	Brain
3 Binah (Understanding)	Divine Understanding	YHWH (Elohim)	Brain
4 Hesed (Lovingkindness)	Compassion	El	Right Arm

Hebrew (English Name)	Quality	God Name	Body Part
5 Gevurah (Strength)	Judgment, Boundaries	Elohim	Left Arm
6 Tiferet (Beauty)	Harmony	YHWH (Adonai)	Heart/Torso
7 Netzach (Victory)	Endurance, Confidence	Adonai Tzevaot	Right Leg/Pelvis
8 Hod (Splendor)	Grace, Vulnerability	Elohim Tzevaot	Left Leg/Pelvis
9 Yesod (Foundation)	Righteousness	Shaddai or El Chai	Sexual Organs
10 Malkhut (Majesty)	Kingdom	Adonai	The Entire Body/Woman

The Tree is a blueprint of us. It represents Creation in theory, while we represent Creation in practice. It is sometimes referred to as Primordial Adam, referring to Adam in thought, the blueprint or prototype of Adam. We, of course, are Adam and Eve in reality. Remember, the sefirot made us in their image and therefore our structure mirrors the structure of the Tree. What goes on in the Tree is mirrored in our world, in our society, in our daily life. The Tree is us. We can show this literally by placing the figure of a man over the Tree. Leonardo da Vinci's famous drawing of a man with his two pairs of arms and two pairs of legs is the perfect model to lay over the Tree. Each sefira corresponds to a part of the body, as depicted in the right-hand column of the chart above. The head of da Vinci's man represents Keter; the top two arms raised higher than the shoulders represent Binah and Hochma; the arms spread at shoulder height represent Gevurah and Hesed; the two legs spread outward represent Hod and Netzach; the genitals represent Yesod; and the two feet planted firmly on the ground are Malkhut. Some Kabbalists say that Malkhut represents the body of the man in its totality, but because Malkhut is also the Shekinah, the feminine presence of God, other Kabbalists see Malkhut in this sense as the female companion to the man represented by the other sefirot together.

All the sefirot worked together to create us, based on a map of how the universe itself was created. Our microcosm fits snugly into the macrocosm of the universe. All human logic, emotions, and relationships are represented somewhere in the Tree. The mixing of the energy among sefirot, picking up qualities here and there and creating new recipes as it goes, results in different situations and emotions played out in our lives. They say, for instance, that history repeats itself. But in truth, nothing repeats. The overall events may appear similar, but the simple fact that time, people, and specific circumstances change, results in what we could call "a very different cake."

The idea that the Tree mirrors the physical world and that the energy from it influences this world has led some people to find links between astrology and Kabbalah. The difference, however, is that Kabbalists don't believe the sefirot control us; they believe that our world is modeled on the sefirot, but our thoughts and actions reverberate back to the sefirot, adding new ingredients to the recipe, so that new situations and consequences are produced. This is crucial to understanding Kabbalah, because Kabbalists believe that we affect change, that it is our actions that repair or prevent repair in the world.

What does this mean in real terms? Life changes and evolves. The world evolves. Things that happen today affect what will happen tomorrow. The people we meet today, the relationships we have, the paths that we take, the choices we make, all determine the paths, choices, and relationships we will have tomorrow—both on an individual level and on a global one. With the continuing evolution of the world, new paths and choices develop. Today, we face situations and events that our great-grandparents never encountered—divorce, social security, HMOs—in the same way that our great-grandparents faced situations we don't see today. Feelings of disconnection and discontent in our society, increased crime rates, and greed today are the direct result of events and choices made in society yesterday. But these are only the negative results. There are also positive aspects of our world today that are the result of decisions and actions taken by people yesterday: health and safety laws that protect us from the spread of disease or dangerous work conditions; better pay for women and family leave plans; recycling and clean-air legislation. The interaction of the forces of the sefirot make our world, but our world continues to stimulate the sefirot to alter the nature of Creation and bring us closer to spiritual awareness.

Take nuclear armament. Twenty years ago it seemed we were on the brink of destruction. Nuclear war between the United States and the Soviet Union seemed inevitable if not imminent. The world teetered on annihilation. But something happened to put it back in balance. Through the work of people like Dr. Helen Caldicott and the Physicians for Social Responsibility, through the labor of diplomats and politicians, and ordinary citizens crusading for sanity, the situation gradually defused. In Tree terms, the forces of Gevurah were leveled off by the forces of Hesed.

When we seek to balance the imbalances in our world, we heal our world. And when we heal imbalances on the micro level, it causes a ripple effect up the Tree to heal the upper worlds as well. In Kabbalah, there are no punishments or rewards, only consequences; actions and reactions. Creation is not a static process. We act, and a ripple of our act flows out from us. Throw a rock in a placid lake and the ripples spread out in even, concentric circles. In this way, our actions ripple through the upper worlds. What occurs in the upper sefirot reflects what occurs in the lower sefirot, but what occurs in the lower sefirot also stimulates change in the upper sefirot, so that the next round of energy that flows down to us is altered. The recipe changes.

Why should we care about how God created the Universe? Kabbalists say we should care because everything that happens on the spiritual plane is a reflection of what happens to us here.

The imbalance, the separation of God depicted in Genesis, is a reflection of the separation in each of us. We are disconnected from God when we do harm to the world and other people, and we are disconnected from ourselves when we do harm to ourselves, when we create an imbalance internally or fail to heal an existing imbalance. Kabbalists tell us that Creation was the act of God removing all elements except judgment from a space in Himself and creating an imbalance in that space. Into this He poured balance. We are meant to mimic that repair.

We are not only created beings, but creating beings, just as the sefirot are creating forces. Human beings are the activators of *tikkun,* who transform the forces of the sefirot and help redirect them back to the source. This requires awareness of our role in the Creation scheme. The ability to repair is in our hands, and we've been given free will to choose what to do with it. Kabbalists say that a kind word or deed travels farther than an evil one. We have the ability to affect great change with the simplest acts of lovingkindness, therefore we have tremendous power. It is left to us to decide what we are going to do with it and how we are going to act.

Repair consists of two types: those that restore the world on the outside—on the physical level—and those that restore it on the inside—the psychological and spiritual levels. The outside is repaired through thoughts, words, and actions; the inside is repaired through developing spiritual awareness by study, meditation, and prayer. If both types work together, there will be good done through conscious intention and awareness. Good deeds have wings that propel them. All good deeds lead to *tikkun*, but Kabbalists say that deeds done in full consciousness and awareness have the greatest effect and accelerate *tikkun*. It's simple; every act that is harmful causes further division in the world, while every act that is healing creates unity. Kabbalah has to do with creating a balanced world on every level, and that includes finding balance within ourselves. One way to achieve this is to unite the divided aspects of ourselves, to balance our physical, intellectual, and spiritual natures.

Kabbalah teaches us that Creation is continuous and is happening now. It teaches us that we can experience Creation today. Once we see the forces in action, and become in tune to them, once we understand the process and our role in it, then we can push up our sleeves and begin the work of repair. That's why the Torah has been called an "owner's manual," because it shows us the way to spiritual development; it shows us from where we originate and how the forces of nature interact to create us and everything else. We don't need to know all the intricacies of Judaism or to understand precisely how the Kabbalists arrived at their beliefs. We simply need to take the next step from what they've given us. We need to put it into practice.

six

PRACTICAL KABBALAH

A human being is part of the whole called by us
"universe," a part limited in time and space. We
experience ourselves, our thoughts and feelings as
something separate from the rest. A kind of optical
delusion of consciousness. This delusion is a kind of
prison for us, restricting us to our personal desires
and to affection for a few persons nearest to us.
Our task must be to free ourselves from the prison
by widening our circle of compassion to embrace
all living creatures and the whole of nature in its
beauty. . . . We shall require a substantially new
manner of thinking if mankind is to survive.

—Albert Einstein

HOW TO APPLY THE LEARNING

We've traced the roots and development of Kabbalah and laid out some of its central tenets; we've examined the

Tree of Life and some of the methods the Kabbalists used to arrive at their beliefs. But how does all of this relate to our daily life? What is the point of all this information, and what do we do with it?

Kabbalah emphasizes that while reading and the pursuit of intellectual knowledge are important for developing awareness and grasping a global view of our world, more important than book learning and teaching are the experiences we have in our daily life. This is where practical Kabbalah can teach us how to apply what we learn in Genesis and the Tree of Life to our personal circumstances, and show us how to begin the practice of healing the world by healing our corner of it. As in Zen practice, it is important to bring the lessons we learn in Kabbalah back to the ground and to put abstract theory into practice.

The term "practical Kabbalah" does not mean the same thing today that it meant to early Kabbalists. Hundreds of years ago, practical Kabbalah referred to white magic that involved a manipulation of the forces of nature for good purposes. When we put the teachings of Kabbalah into practice today, however, there is no magic or the conjuring of forces involved; but the effect is still the same. Practical Kabbalah has been described as a system of ethics that focuses on a right way of living in community, though with the higher goals of affecting positive change in the universe and of drawing us closer to God (what Kabbalists refer to as "cleaving" to God) through spiritual awareness and the elevation of the physical world to the spiritual one. We don't simply get closer to God through meditation and prayer, we draw closer to Him through actions and thoughts that recognize the connectedness of all the universe and that recognize the existence of God in everything in that universe.

When we lead a Kabbalistic life, we not only have a positive effect on the physical world, but our actions also have a soothing effect on the forces above that in turn cause alterations in the energy that flows down to us and surrounds us. When we commit acts of lovingkindness, they reverberate throughout the spiritual world and help heal or correct the universe. Thus, we not only heal our neighbors and make them feel better, we heal ourselves as well and heal the God in exile.

Opportunities to heal the world abound and are presented to us every day and every moment; we just have to open our eyes to them. Healing the world generally doesn't require monumental actions on our part—although occasionally these kinds of acts are needed too—but rather simple, mundane tasks that help mend the rifts that separate us from each other. It can be a simple matter of running an errand for a neighbor or thanking a secretary for a job well done—tasks that require no great energy on our part—or it can be a matter of controlling our anger against someone who has scratched our car in the parking lot or taken our place in the movie line. It can involve delivering meals to AIDS patients or swallowing criticism of our spouses; or it can be a matter of speaking out against injustices or campaigning for political reform.

Evolution in the larger picture first requires evolution in the smaller one. Focusing first on changing and repairing the separate parts of our own life changes and repairs the bigger picture that contains all of us. It's similar to building a jigsaw puzzle of the Grand Canyon. The whole picture is too vast to do at one time, so you begin with one corner of the puzzle and first match all of the pieces that contain rose-colored rock; then you put together all of the pieces of the river that runs the length of the canyon. All of the small scenes that you complete add up to the larger picture. Thus putting the puzzle together section by section builds the larger picture simultaneously.

WORKING THE TREE

Practical Kabbalah revolves around "working the Tree"; that is, studying the various parts of the Tree, the various aspects of each sefira, to see what they tell us about our life and our world. For example, the qualities that define Binah (Understanding) teach us something about knowledge between good and bad, and therefore about repentance and the importance of making reparations for our actions. By passing from one sefira to another, we gain awareness of different aspects of our world and our being that help us repair the rift between the physical and spiritual worlds. When we raise our level of awareness, the gap between these two levels narrows. The more conscious we are of our connection to other people and to God, the less we will act in ways that are separate from them.

We can divide the work of the Tree into two kinds: internal work and external work. Internal work is the work we do on ourselves, on our thoughts and intentions and our perceptions of the world, to help change the way we act in it. This involves seeing the connection between things in the universe, but it also involves being aware of why we think and act the way we do. If we understand, for instance, that our false perceptions of the world and other people as separate from us lead us to treat them with disrespect and lack of compassion, we can alter our behavior. Internal work also involves balancing the male and female aspects inside us, such as developing and giving attention to both our assertive and nurturing characteristics, as well as balancing our intellectual and rational nature with our subjective, experiential side. All aspects of us have their moments of domination—there are times in our life or even moments of our day when we are confident and assertive, and other times when we are thoughtful or insecure. The goal is a holistic one of integrating all these aspects, to exercise all the muscles of our personality and character, so that we become a whole being.

External work is how we put our new perceptions into practice; how we begin to act once we see the world in its connectedness. Our actions, in order to have the greatest effect in the upper world, have to occur on three levels: on the intellectual, on the spiritual, and on the physical. This means that our thoughts (intellect) and intentions (soul or heart) must match the act. It is not enough to just perform a good deed, we have to want to do good by the deed and have the intent to heal the world through the deed. For this reason we have free will. Someone who commits a good deed because he is commanded to do so is still doing good in the world, but not in the same way as someone who does it with the fullness of his heart, with complete commitment, and with knowledge and understanding of the fact that he doesn't necessarily have to do it. Furthermore, to simply do something without really being aware of what we are doing is not the same as having full consciousness of what we are doing. This is what gives an act "wings" and elevates it to a higher level, makes the good energy soar up the Tree.

We will begin our examination of the Tree with Keter and work our way down, but you don't have to begin your work at the top of the Tree; you can start at the bottom with Malkhut and examine each sefira on your way up. It makes sense to climb up, since the highest levels of development are at the top of the Tree and since Kabbalists tell us that Malkhut, the last sefira on the bottom, is the "gate" to the paths of wisdom. It is through Malkhut that we enter the realm of wisdom. Once you have examined all the sefirot, however, you can focus on any sefira as you experience imbalances in your life.

One caveat before we go on: It might seem at times that the sefirot contradict each other. For instance, we are told that we have tremendous power, but that we should also feel as if we have no power. We should strive to have no harshness and our face should be filled with joy, but we should know that anger and evil are also parts of God. Taken as a whole, the Tree presents a balanced picture of existence. But when only parts of the Tree are emphasized in our life or in the world, then the balance is off. The goal of working each sefira is to achieve overall balance. This concept is similar to that of Eastern healing practices, which seek to find balance in the body by working on various areas until energy moves freely through all parts of the body. Kabbalists see our bodies as sacred vessels, like the sefirot, that receive God's energy. When we are unbalanced—for instance, when we spend too much time developing our physical body at the expense of our mind—we are like cracked vessels; our ability to receive and hold the energy is impaired. But when we are balanced—when we apply appropriate levels of energy to care for our mind, body, and soul—the energy has no obstacles to keep it from flowing freely. The aim is to find the balance in ourselves and in our world; to know when to apply lovingkindness and when to hold back; to know when ambition is an appropriate and beneficial quality, and to understand when it crosses the line into obsession.

KETER

The lesson that Keter teaches us is one of humility. Humility is the quality associated with Keter because in Keter the "I" does not exist. There is only the No-Thing, because there is no differentiation here. It is the absence of ego and the presence of a being that is greater than any one of us alone. Humility is the

158

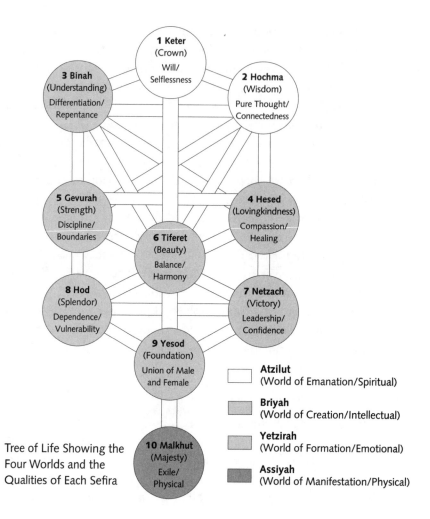

1 Keter
(Crown)
Will/
Selflessness

3 Binah
(Understanding)
Differentiation/
Repentance

2 Hochma
(Wisdom)
Pure Thought/
Connectedness

5 Gevurah
(Strength)
Discipline/
Boundaries

4 Hesed
(Lovingkindness)
Compassion/
Healing

6 Tiferet
(Beauty)
Balance/
Harmony

8 Hod
(Splendor)
Dependence/
Vulnerability

7 Netzach
(Victory)
Leadership/
Confidence

9 Yesod
(Foundation)
Union of Male
and Female

10 Malkhut
(Majesty)
Exile/
Physical

Atzilut
(World of Emanation/Spiritual)

Briyah
(World of Creation/Intellectual)

Yetzirah
(World of Formation/Emotional)

Assiyah
(World of Manifestation/Physical)

Tree of Life Showing the
Four Worlds and the
Qualities of Each Sefira

recognition that the world is bigger than you or me; it is recognition of the No-thingness in you. The Kabbalists are not saying to be nothing, but to abandon the personae you've developed, to throw away the ego and the person you think you are, to get at the core of who you really are. You are not the physical being that you think you are, you are a part of God. Keter tells us to release the poses and the images we project to the world and recognize that in our essence we are not the powerful businessman or movie star, nor are we the secretary or the computer analyst or the landscape gardener. We are these things on the outside, but inside we are something else. Kabbalists say that to make room for God, you need to empty yourself of you. Creation is the process through which nothingness becomes the I. When we are talking about returning to the state of Keter we are talking about a state in which the I becomes the "no thing" in which we don't see ourselves as apart from God or the world. Gershom Scholem points out that the same letters that form the Hebrew word for "I," *ani—aleph-yud-nun—*also form the Hebrew word for "nothing," *ain.* Rearrange the letters, and we are transported to the realm of nothingness.

Humility is recognizing your lowliness. Even Keter, which is the closest to Ein Sof of all the sefirot, is not Ein Sof. So no matter how high up you get, Keter tells us, you are still below Ein Sof. You are knee-high to a grasshopper in cosmic terms. This doesn't mean, however, that you are worthless. Humility is not about annulling and voiding yourself and "giving your power over" to other people. We are not meant to be mousy or slink around the office because we think we don't matter. On the contrary, we matter a lot. It's just that we matter no more or no less than the postal worker who weighs our package, the IRS accountant who does our audit, the teenager who delivers our paper, or the millionaire who runs the computer empire. Keter is about selflessness, but it's also about remembering that if the other person is important, if the other person is divine, so am I.

Keter is also about accepting your victories graciously and not letting the praises of other people place you above Creation. Remember your place, Keter tells us from the top of the Tree. But humility also comes from recognizing your faults and your failures and realizing that you are not a perfect being. It comes from accepting these faults as part of who you are; recognizing that you are composed of many parts, none of them good or bad on their own. It comes down to accepting who you are; and that who you are is a spark of the divine, which has the capability of good and evil in it.

In the end, Keter tells us to treat every being as if he or she is God, because they are. We all stem from Nothingness, and we all return to Nothingness as well.

One way in which we can tap into our connection to the realm of No-thingness is to do a meditation in which we imagine the flow of energy that runs down through the sefirot into us, envelops us with all its light, then returns to follow a path up the Tree back to Keter. To do this simple meditation, begin by sitting quietly in a comfortable space with the lights turned out, close your eyes, and breathe. Just breathe in and out and direct your mind to your breath. Follow your breath in and out without trying to control or regulate it. If distracting thoughts arise and pull your mind away from your breath, acknowledge the thoughts, but then gently bring your mind back to your breath. Once you feel your body relax, you can begin by imagining the Tree of Life, with a flow of white light or energy emanating from the top of the Tree. Imagine this white light as something warm and energizing. Watch it flow gently down from Keter to each of the sefirot below, from Hochma to Binah, from Hesed to Gevurah, illuminating each vessel as it fills and overflows it. Then imagine the white light pouring out of Malkhut into you and enveloping you in its warm, unconditional embrace. Sit with this feeling for a few minutes, and when you feel you've received enough of the light, imagine sending part of the light out of you and back up the Tree, through each of the sefirot, until it arrives back at Keter and flows into the source of light that is still pouring out of Keter. Imagine the light as ever-flowing from above and ever-flowing through you. When you feel energized and relaxed, you can bring yourself out of the meditation by gently returning your mind to your breath. Focus your attention on your in-breath and then your out-breath for a minute or so, again not trying to control the breath in any way. And when you're ready, slowly open your eyes.

From Hochma, Kabbalists tell us we should develop an under-standing of our connection to all things above and below—to God and to everything else in the world. Hochma is the first of the sefirot to receive from Keter, and it then turns around to give to Binah. Hochma represents the notion of wholeness and connectedness with all the things in Creation. If we feel con-nected to all things, then we tend to treat things as if they were not separate from us, and we feel compassion for all beings. As a consequence, Kabbalists teach that we should not kill or harm any plant or animal unless it is absolutely necessary for our sus-tenance. One may kill an animal for food, if necessary, but the killing must be done with full consciousness that the animal is connected to us and connected to God.

When we eat, we eat with the awareness that the food has come from God and that it is serving a purpose to nourish us. Some people believe the Kabbalists are actually advocating veg-etarianism or the steps to vegetarianism, and that if someone is truly mindful of the animal they are eating, they won't want to eat it. But the early Kabbalists didn't make this final leap, al-though they may very well have been implying it.

Either way, the Kabbalists tell us that when we sit down to eat we should first take a moment to reflect on the role of the plant or animal in the universe as well as our own role. We could call Hochma the sefira of Thanksgiving. We acknowledge the divine spark in the things that God has provided us. At the same time that we acknowledge this, we also elevate the food to a spiritual level, acknowledging it as part of the divine Creation. All of this serves as a reminder that we are not the masters of our world and that we do not therefore have the right to treat the world as if it were our property by killing animals for sport, dumping chemicals in rivers, or depleting natural resources. While we may have in Creation a special role that plants and animals do not have, it would be harmful to the world and ourselves to abuse that power.

One way we can live in Hochma consciousness is to be thankful for what we do have. When we go to sleep at night we can do it with the grateful consciousness that we have a roof over our head and a warm bed to sleep in. One exercise for experiencing Hochma consciousness is to take time to appreciate the good things in your life. Focus on what you have and what you are grateful for, whether it be the people in your life, a fulfilling job, a reliable baby-sitter, or an understanding boss. Think about—perhaps even make a list—of all of the things that make you feel good, and focus on this feeling. You might even go the extra step and thank a person who has made you feel good.

We can be thankful for our friendships by taking the time to express our gratefulness for having friends in our life. You can tell your mother that you are thankful for all she has taught you. Of course it is difficult to live in Hochma consciousness all the time, just as it is difficult to live constantly in any state of consciousness. This is not the goal. To remain constant in anything is not natural for human beings nor for the universe. The Tree teaches us that Creation is dynamic; our lives and relationships are dynamic as well. And there will be times when we won't feel grateful for what we have; when the food we eat is devoid of taste and pleasure; when our children annoy us or don't do what we ask them to do; or when our mother interferes in affairs where she's not welcome. And there are times when we simply don't have anything to be grateful for—when someone we love dies or is struck with painful disease; when a relationship ends and all we can feel is the pain. At times like these we don't feel connected to other people; we feel alone and abandoned and victimized, and it feels unnatural to be grateful. But Kabbalists say that feeling grateful is what connects us to people and to life. Often, if we are feeling despair, we are seeing what we don't have rather than what we do have; Kabbalists say that if we see how the world is connected, then we cannot feel lonely. When we see how God has provided for us—whether with a roof over our head, a handout when we are poor, or a simple kindness when we feel defeated—then we cannot feel abandoned.

BINAH

Binah teaches us about returning to oneness, because Binah is the sefira at which the emanation from Ein Sof becomes refracted. Within Binah, however, everything is still whole. Kabbalists say that Binah is as high as we can reach, that beyond it there is no "I," and that it is therefore impossible for us to imagine or know the region above.

In chapter 5, we discussed repentance and how it was built into Creation so that Adam and Eve could return to God after straying from Him. Since return and repentance are closely tied, in Binah we meditate on repentance. Binah teaches us about wholeness and about the idea that we are connected to everyone else and are all on the same mission, though our individual routes may be different. But to achieve repentance on the larger level, we have to start on the smaller level and think about the things that we've done that have caused harm.

Therefore, in Binah we examine what we've done to harm someone else. For Kabbalists, this examination can be a daily task that we conduct at the end of each day, taking an account of our actions and words throughout the previous hours. Once we begin to do this, we may find ourselves stopping before we commit an act that we know we will have to account for in the evening. If another has done something to harm us during that day, we can also take the time before going to bed to contemplate our feelings about the action and then release the person from our hurt. Sometimes this cannot be accomplished in one day if the hurt is especially deep or ongoing, but in the case of minor injuries this exercise can help us clean the slate, approach the person with fresh eyes, and avoid perpetuating any further injury out of revenge.

Binah is a sefira that is particularly suited to a meditation practice because it focuses on something tangible, such as a wrong action. One way to contemplate and elevate our mistakes is to meditate on a specific thing we did and try to transform its energy by learning from it. To meditate on repentance, you might simply start a regular meditation practice to relax and focus your thoughts, like the one described in the Keter section. Once you feel ready, you can then think about something you've done, either in the past or earlier in the day, that you know was wrong or that you know hurt someone else. Try to recall how you were feeling at the time you did it. Were you angry or frightened? Were you thinking about something that happened earlier in the day, or something this person said or did previously that you have not forgiven? Were you directing misplaced anger toward someone else on this person?

Now try to imagine the thoughts and feelings of this person at the time you hurt them. Try to imagine the perspective of the person on the receiving end. Are they surprised or hurt? Are they angry by your action? Have you caused them upset in any way?

Once you have examined the hurt from both sides, imagine the two of you being surrounded by the energy of acceptance and lovingkindness. Perhaps you might envision it as the arms of a warm and loving parent who envelops you both. Imagine the forgiveness and healing energy pulsing into the two of you, and feel the connection between you and the other person through the arms of this parent.

Now put yourself back into the same situation and imagine how you might have handled the situation differently. Imagine yourself undoing the wrong—perhaps taking a breath before you speak or walking away instead of reacting. See whether you can envision yourself acting in a different way that acknowledges both your feelings and your connection to the other person. Then examine how this different way of acting makes you feel, and how it makes the other person feel. You may experience a sense of calm and peacefulness at having watched yourself right the wrong.

Once you feel you have worked through the incident, you can bring yourself back by returning to your breath. Place your attention on watching the in-breath become the out-breath. Just follow your breathing like this for several minutes, then when you are ready, slowly open your eyes.

This exercise is not intended to create feelings of guilt; it's simply to allow you to look at an event outside of the emotions that surrounded it when it occurred. At the time you performed the action, maybe you were in a state of mind in which you couldn't think of an alternative action; maybe you were unaware that what you would do would cause harm; or maybe you wanted to get back at the other person for something they did to you. But now, looking back on the incident from the perspective of Binah and Hochma, perhaps you see your act in a different light and see how everything we do is an opportunity for growth. We all make mistakes, and we all hurt people, sometimes unintentionally and sometimes intentionally. The point is not to chastise ourselves for this, but to become aware of what we do so that the next time we are in a similar situation, we can pull back from the emotion and watch what we are doing. Often it is not enough to want to act differently; we first have to be fully aware of what is going on inside us. We have to recognize the fears and insecurities that lead us to act in harmful ways, and once we can identify these, we can begin to change our behavior. With such an understanding, you can then imagine yourself in the same situation, but this time acting in a different way that acknowledges your connection to the other person and that acknowledges your oneness and their oneness with God. You might feel a sense of relief or a sense of cleansing when you see that you have the power to act differently.

This is what repentance is about; it's about transforming our mistakes into lessons and it's about being aware of our behavior and seeing it in the context of the larger picture. The goal is to begin to act from that sense of wholeness and connectedness that we get from Hochma and Binah. Returning to wholeness, *teshuva,* begins with repentance of our individual actions, because once we become aware of how our actions affect all of Creation, we can't help but think differently before we act the next time.

Hesed is lovingkindness and refers to the total outflowing of unconditional love from God. When we exhibit lovingkindness, we heal the world because acts of lovingkindness bring unification. We exhibit lovingkindness when we have mercy and compassion and empathy for the suffering of other people. We are in a Hesed consciousness when we care for the sick and elderly, nurture a child, or give charity. Healing is accomplished through our relationships with other people. When you take care of a sick person or give comfort to someone in pain, you are at the same time giving comfort to all of Creation, and the act continues beyond the particular moment. Not long ago, my father, a man chivalrous to his bones, stopped to help a female motorist who was stranded along the roadside. When she asked what she could do to repay him, he told her, "Just tell your husband that if he ever sees a woman motorist along the roadside to please stop and help her because she may be my wife or daughter." Indeed, a few weeks later I found myself stranded on the roadside with a smoking engine, and a gentleman my father's age stopped to assist me. When he stepped out of his car he told me, "I don't know why I stopped; I never do, but I saw you standing there and decided to pull over."

Charity is an act of lovingkindness, and it is possible to give charity in many ways other than through the obvious donations.

You might arrange with your eye doctor to purchase a new pair of reading glasses for a needy patient, or offer to take an elderly neighbor grocery shopping once a week. You might offer to baby-sit for friends who can't afford to hire a sitter. A friend of mine once arranged anonymously to pay the overdue day care bills for another friend who was having financial difficulties. But charity is not just about what we give materially, it's about how we give ourselves as well. Ultimately, this is the greatest charity, because it involves human interaction and the giving of our hearts rather than what can be the sterile giving of money and possessions.

You never really know the effect your actions and words have on other people or on the world. A simple courtesy such as opening the door for a mother whose arms are loaded with a screaming child might be enough to calm her nerves so that she can then respond to her child in a patient and soothing manner. It is said that good deeds bring forth life and bad deeds hasten death. Think about it: when someone treats us with love and kindness it lightens our heart, and when they treat us with disdain it makes us feel heavy and defeated. The world is already full of so much suffering that any kindness has the ability to cross great distances and affect many people.

But Hesed is not only about giving, it's also about receiving, and about your own ability to receive what others give to you. If other people try to help you but you refuse that help, then you are not working in balance. It's a two-way street, and that's why balancing Hesed is about knowing your own boundaries and respecting the boundaries of others. It's about knowing what you need and being able to accept it when it's offered; it's also about asking other people for what they need and being willing to give it.

Another aspect of Hesed is related to the unconditional love that God gives us. During times of suffering, we should remember the blessings of God and give back to Him the unconditional love that He gives us. It's one of the most difficult concepts on the Tree, because the Kabbalists are asking that during the times when we feel the least capable of seeing the good in our life, we should reaffirm God's goodness and recognize that He only gives us suffering out of love and in order to help us learn. The Kabbalists are not saying that suffering is not suffering. They are saying that just as the fall of Adam and Eve was an act of love to help them learn, the sufferings in our life usually contain blessings or lessons to help us grow and become stronger. When someone we love suffers and dies and we want to curse God, it is that moment exactly, Kabbalist say, when we should recall the goodness of God. When we've lost our job and are going through a divorce, when all seems lost, we need to remember that it really isn't. Ultimately, the foundation is still there. We still have God.

We've all heard about people who suffer great setbacks and yet seem to bend in the wind like the reeds. I remember reading an interview with a famous writer who had just lost her home in a fire that burned for days and consumed hundreds of homes in the hills of Oakland, California, in 1991. She had lost everything, including the nearly completed manuscript of her next novel. And yet her conclusion about the loss was that it was a great adventure. She'd write the novel again, she said, and maybe this time it would reveal itself to her in a different way. In the same fire was a renowned photographer of advanced age who had lost a houseful of irreplaceable negatives and prints, the culmination of his life's work. By chance, however, some of his photos had been away at a museum that was organizing an exhibition of his work. For him also the experience was a freeing one. It somehow liberated him to begin fresh (and he was seventy or eighty years old). He said that he didn't realize it until after the fire that the pictures had been in part a burden because they had defined his life. Now he was free to redefine it.

The Kabbalists are not suggesting that we give in to suffering, that we accept bad things as the will of God, or that we allow injustices to occur because there must be a reason for them. Nor do they suggest that we not give a sick child medical care because we think it is the will of God that the child grew ill in the first place. They are simply saying that if God is all things, then He is the good things *and* He is the bad things. God gives us only the pain and suffering that He knows we can handle, and he gives it to us as a tool for growth. If you can go beyond the suffering itself and see a lesson in it, then you can transform it into something good and useful. And if within the suffering you can find meaning, then you may also perhaps make the suffering more bearable. It's a matter of acknowledging the suffering, but then asking ourselves, What do I do now? We are given choices. Every difficult situation presents us with an opportunity. We can look at suffering as something unbearable and unfair, or we can look at it as an opportunity to learn.

This is not to suggest that the person dying of cancer is not doing his part if he doesn't think about the good things that come from his suffering or the suffering of his family. Kabbalists do not say that we should turn away from someone else's suffering or even from our own, but to look at the suffering and see if there is anything that it can teach us. Is there some way that it can be turned around? Does the illness bring an estranged family together? Does it make others value their life more? None of this detracts from the suffering of the person who is ill; none of it devalues their suffering. But is there anything at all to be taken away from the suffering?

Think about something in your life that is causing you to suffer, and try to see if there is a lesson in it or some hidden blessing. At its most basic level, the blessing in suffering is that it allows us to appreciate our blessings. Without the curses in our life, without the suffering and the challenges, we would not appreciate and recognize the times when these things are absent from our life.

If Hesed is the desire to give, Gevurah is the desire to obtain, to acquire; it is ambition, it is the source of creative and artistic energy and the impetus to invent and discover new things. If Hesed is the outflowing of love and endless giving, then Gevurah is borders and laws and definitions. The power behind Gevurah is what holds a society together and gets things accomplished. It ensures that we have houses that are safe to live in and food that is safe to eat. Gevurah also ensures that the species continues, because without Gevurah there would be no sexual activity, no desire. It is the source of our drive and energy, the will to change things and make things better.

Gevurah is also about restraint and moderation. Kabbalah doesn't want to eradicate or repress our desires. However, we do need to balance them and know when desires are appropriate and when they aren't. When they are laid out in front of us where we can see them, then they have less power over us. When they are repressed and deep in our subconscious, then they work their way up to the surface in a manner that may be less controllable. Take the wind out of the sails of your evil inclinations, Kabbalists seem to say, by addressing them first and not denying they exist.

As with any quality on the Tree, Gevurah applied for the wrong reasons leads to abuse of power. Sexuality and pleasure in food, art, nature, in the enjoyment of a good joke, all come with the gift package of Creation, but these gifts are to be used wisely. Kabbalists say that pleasure is really the spiritual making its presence known in our world. When we enjoy something, we are experiencing its spiritual nature. But everything has its place, and everything is good when it is moderated by its balancing trait. Inappropriate lust that leads us to cheat on a spouse or partner; jealousy that moves us to destroy what someone else has instead of motivating us to achieve something we want—these are examples of Gevurah out of balance.

To experience a Gevurah consciousness, Kabbalists advise us to examine areas of our life that are out of balance by excessive attention to them—eating too much or watching too much TV. There are plenty of ways in which we can introduce discipline into our life to help balance these areas of excessiveness. You might start by making a list of the things you've intended to do or need to accomplish, as well as a list of all the things you spend your time doing instead of these things; then you can create a program that gradually reduces the excessive activity and focuses on completing the things you want to accomplish. For instance, if we spend too much time watching TV or reading romance novels instead of being with our family or attending to responsibilities, we might want to reduce the time engaged in these activities. Instead of eating a bag of potato chips as an evening snack, we might want to opt for something healthier or even a trip to the gym. If our evenings are spent on the telephone with friends, we might want to make only one phone call a night and limit it to half an hour; then spend the remainder of the evening pursuing a course we want to take or helping our kids with homework. If we go to the gym every night, we might decide to drop one night a week from the schedule and pursue a different interest or meet with friends. There are myriad ways in which we introduce imbalance into our lives, either through habit or laziness, and attention to this imbalance is one of the first steps we can take to correct it.

On the external side, Gevurah establishes boundaries in our relationships with other people and finds the balance to giving. If you are drained of energy because you give too freely, or if you feel that people take advantage of you, then you need to establish boundaries. Boundaries are necessary not only in your life but in the world at large. If you spend too much time trying to solve the problems of other people, then pull back and take time for yourself. If you cook dinner each night for your family, ask someone else to take over one or two nights a week; delegate responsibilities and chores to other family members; say No when you need to say No, and don't feel guilty about it.

TIFERET

Tiferet symbolizes harmony and balance and is at the center of the Tree of Life for a reason. Too much of one thing is never good. Even too much of a good thing is too much. That's why we have tough love, the balance of Hesed with Gevurah. This is harmony on the cosmic level. On the individual level, harmony and balance exist in the personality when we unify the lovingkindness and severity within us.

When Tiferet is balanced it is actually not perfectly balanced, but leans a little toward the side of Hesed, toward lovingkindness. Why is this? Because the universe began with an act of judgment, with the concentration of Din, and therefore there is slightly more Din in the world than there is Hesed. We need to balance the severity inherent in our world with a bit more mercy and compassion in order to achieve true balance. A world with a little more Hesed gives us leeway to have Din without it being destructive. We need a slight reserve of Hesed to balance the greater weight of Din in the world. We could also look at it another way. Din is the gravitational force that pulls us downward, that pulls us away from God; we need the thrust of a little extra mercy to overcome this downward pull in order to propel us back up. An equal force of mercy will just keep us in place, but the extra rocket boost of mercy will lift us back in the direction we need to go.

Tiferet is not only about finding the balance between two things, it's about bringing two things together. Making peace between two individuals is also a divine act, because it symbolizes the union of exiled parts of God. To make peace between feuding siblings, old friends, between colleagues or a husband and wife are all acts of unification that reverberate in the divine realm. This is a *tikkun;* it repairs what is torn and unites what is apart. To practice Tiferet consciousness, then, is to find ways to balance giving and receiving and to mend rifts. If two colleagues are at odds over competing ideas, see if you can find a compromise that combines both their suggestions. If friends or neighbors are estranged from one another, or if you are estranged from a friend yourself, try to find some way to mend the rift and restore the relationship.

NETZACH

The Kabbalist understanding of the qualities of the next two sefirot is never as clear as the other ones on the Tree. But I would suggest that these two sefirot are about dominance and dependence as well as about thoughts and emotions. As mentioned in chapter 5, Netzach is about self-confidence and esteem and assuming leadership. Netzach represents a position of power and can sometimes lean toward a position of dominance. We are experiencing Netzach when we assume a position of leadership or when we take care of a child or are involved in teaching. One of the ways, then, in which we can develop Netzach consciousness is to offer our knowledge or services to someone who might benefit from them; for instance, we might offer to tutor someone in a language or teach someone how to play the piano. If we are an accountant, we might offer to help someone with their tax return, or if we are a gardener we might help someone plant a garden.

But with regard to our internal life, Netzach is also about our feelings and emotions. Kabbalists talk about Hesed (Lovingkindness) and Gevurah (Strength) being supported by Netzach (Victory) and Hod (Splendor). Therefore, how we act is often determined by how we think and feel. If we are angry at someone, or even at the world, we are less likely to want to be kind to that person or offer them compassion. Netzach represents our emotional nature and how we express data that we take in from the world and then respond to the world. It is the place from which we act out of feeling rather than out of thought. Hod, on the other hand, represents our thoughts—the part of us that puts the reins on emotions and keeps them in balance. The way to achieve wholeness is to balance the two so that we are neither governed wholly by our emotions nor wholly by our thoughts.

Emotions are good things. They lead us to have compassion for other people, they lead us to have passion for life, and they lead us to make changes in areas of our life that feel painful. But unbalanced emotion can lead to too much passion, such as out-of-control anger. Some anger is appropriate, of course, but much of our anger is unnecessary. It is connected to other feelings and emotions that are stored inside our subconscious and cause us to interpret the innocent actions of other people in negative ways. Kabbalists aren't suggesting that we repress emotions. Instead they're suggesting we acknowledge their existence and figure out where they're coming from, and then learn how to deal with them. Once you recognize anger and acknowledge it, you need to decide whether or not to act on it.

Acknowledging our anger instead of repressing it is a recipe for psychological health, because we know that a person who represses feelings and emotions, who denies that he has anger and desire and jealousy, is more enslaved by these emotions than the person who recognizes that they exist but manages to deal with them in constructive ways. Suppression is not the way of Kabbalah, although moderation in all things is.

Thoughts and emotions come and go and change. Recognizing this is important for dealing with them. Awareness of when we have emotions and what triggers them leads us to realize that we are not our emotions and feelings, and they are not us. We have a range of responses we can choose from—after all, we have free will. We can choose to act on anger, but also need to be ready for the consequences of that anger and to know whether or not they are the consequences we want. Some emotions we can just observe quietly, as we do with our breath in meditation. We can take note of them and watch them but not act on them. This is the type of control that is beneficial. It's not about denying anything; it's not about punishing ourselves for having anger, it's simply about seeing anger but choosing not to act on it. We don't have to scream at the guy who cuts us off on the freeway or fume at the person who insists on writing a check in the "cash only" line.

One of the meditations recommended for Netzach is to practice breathing in patience and breathing out lovingkindness. In this way, the Kabbalist path is similar to the Buddhist one. When we "breathe in patience" we allow enough time for anger to subside. When we observe the pattern of our emotions, we begin to know ourselves better and know when an emotion is a passing one and should simply be patted on the head like a small child who needs attention, and also when it should be addressed. Furthermore, Kabbalists say that if we do express anger, we should not let it linger, because then anger loses its beneficial quality and becomes destructive. To hold a grudge is an example of this; to give someone the silent treatment is also a response that doesn't heal.

Anger can be positive if it addresses a legitimate injustice. A *real* injustice, that is—not simply the inconvenience of being issued a $230 parking ticket for using the commuter lane for what *we* thought was an emergency. We're talking about the anger of people who are oppressed or beaten or are in some way innocent victims. We're talking about the kind of passionate anger that compels good change.

But even then, we need to take care that the anger doesn't control and consume us and thereby do more harm than good. There are people who are legitimately angry for things that have been done to them, but then they let the anger fester. There are people who power their anger into crusades that may ultimately cause good change in society but throw their own emotional balance out of whack. A couple of years ago, Dr. Helen Caldicott was interviewed on national radio about her work with the nuclear disarmament issue, and she spoke about the damaging effect her work had on her marriage and her relationship to her children. We've all heard about people who, powered by anger and a sense of injustice, throw themselves into causes to save the whales or the starving children in Ethiopia—both good causes—but in the process neglect their own families or treat other people worse than the animals they save.

One exercise for dealing with anger when it arises is to just sit quietly with it and watch it. Rather than react, we can try to pull back and look at the anger and examine it; try to understand what is making us angry. Sometimes it's not a specific incident that makes us angry, but our physical exhaustion that makes us unable to respond positively to the people around us. We also have to understand that we decide what makes us angry; the actions and words of other people have less power to make us angry than we have to *allow* them to make us angry. Sitting with the anger and taking some deep breaths can help us figure out how to respond in a more relaxed manner.

HOD

If Netzach is dominance and power, then Hod is dependence. Hod is the child that requires care and nurturing, as well as teaching. We are in a Hod state when we seek learning from someone more knowledgeable than us or seek assistance from someone who can help us. Some of the ways to experience Hod consciousness are to read books or take a course or to ask a friend to teach us a skill that they possess.

In counterbalance to Netzach, Hod also represents our thoughts, which often lead to the emotions we have and to our actions. For instance, it may be thoughts of worthlessness or inferiority that lead us to withdraw from people or imagine slights that don't exist. It may be fears about our partner leaving us that make us depressed and unable to act freely in the relationship. Thoughts have the ability to lead us into all kinds of trouble because we assign them so much power. We think that if we have a thought, then it must be true. And we think that if we have a thought, then we must act on it. If we believe that our neighbor doesn't care about us, then we imagine that the noise he makes is done on purpose. If we think that a colleague is smarter than we are, then we might imagine that the colleague is out to get our job. If we think we cannot affect change in the world or in our life, then it can lead us to despair and inactivity. If we think that other people are talking behind our back, it might lead us to gossip about them in return.

The way to deal with thoughts is to sit quietly with them, as with emotions, and evaluate their validity. Negative thoughts, particularly, have a way of defeating us and gnawing at our self-esteem and equilibrium. One way to examine our thoughts is to keep track during the day of the kinds of thoughts we have, depending on what we want to deal with. For instance, if we feel angry at a colleague, we might keep track of all our thoughts during the day about that colleague. If we feel hostility toward our husband or children, we might keep a list of all the thoughts that come to our mind about what prompts us to feel hostile.

This is not an exercise for making a case against the person; it simply allows us to label the thoughts and get them down so we can examine them. Once we have them in writing, we can begin to examine the validity of the thoughts more accurately and to analyze why we have them. Then, when we take into account what the rest of Kabbalah teaches us about our connections to other people and our need for committing acts of lovingkindness, we can tear the paper up and release the thoughts of their power.

YESOD

Yesod is the foundation of the Tree. It is the trunk upon which the upper sefirot stand. If Tiferet is the male and Malkhut is the female, Yesod is the point of union between the two. Kabbalists talk about Yesod as being the place where the seed is stored; therefore Yesod is symbolic of the male genitals. Kabbalists view sexual relations between a man and woman as a symbolic union of Tiferet and Malkhut; it is the physical union of male and female but it is also the symbolic union of everything in the universe that is separated or in exile. Kabbalists believe that sexual union between a man and woman is the greatest union of all, because on every level the union achieves harmony, including harmony between the physical and spiritual.

If Yesod is the union between the male and female, we experience Yesod consciousness when we achieve balance between the two aspects of ourselves that represent male and female qualities, when we develop our nurturing capabilities as well as our leadership capabilities. We might achieve balance in this sense by looking for ways in which to develop the gender aspect in ourselves that is less formed. For instance, we might learn how to fix a car or work with carpentry or do anything that would develop our independence and strength. Instead of giving our finances to someone else to take care of, we might opt to learn about them for ourselves. On the other hand, we might want to learn how to cook or give a massage or do any other nurturing activities such as taking care of a child for someone or listening to a friend.

MALKHUT

Much of what this sefira tells us lies in its position on the Tree. Malkhut teaches us to be humble, to remember that we are on the bottom rung of the ladder, in fact we are lower than the bottom rung because we are actually below Malkhut. Malkhut is at the top of our world, but at the bottom of the world above. Malkhut reminds us that no matter how much power we have here on earth, no matter how many highrise buildings we own and private jets and movie deals we have, we are still at the bottom of the universe.

Malkhut represents the roots. It is through the roots that a tree takes in much of its nourishment, and it is through Malkhut that we experience the world and take in all our data about it. Via the physical senses—sight, hearing, smell, touch, taste—we take in information about the world that we then process through our subconscious (symbolized by Yesod) to develop thoughts and emotions (symbolized by Netzach and Hod) about what we experience. From our thoughts and emotions and subconscious come the impetus for many of our actions and beliefs.

This is from the bottom looking up. But looking down from the top, we see that Malkhut only gets the light or energy of Ein Sof from the sefirot above it. We could say that the sefirot above are the leaves that collect the light, and through photosynthesis they turn the data received from below into the world that we then experience. We said earlier that our actions affect the recipe above, causing the sefirot to interact in different ways with one another and produce the world that we then experience. As it says in the Zohar, "From below must come the impulse to move the power above. Thus, to form the cloud, vapor ascends first from earth. . . . It is from below that the movement starts, and thereafter is all perfected. If the [community] failed to initiate the impulse, the One above would also not move to go to her, and it is thus the yearning from below which brings about the completion above." It is through our actions in the lower end of the universe that evolution is initiated, because it is through our world that change is initiated. While God makes His presence known in the world constantly, it is only in our willingness to see it and make contact with it that spiritual connection can occur.

When the Tree is in balance, the energy flow from above is smooth and unheeded. But when the Tree is out of balance, the energy begins to pool on one side of the Tree and become imbalanced. When we act rightly, the flow of energy comes down to Malkhut to nourish her.

Malkhut sits in a position of exile. Exile means loneliness; it means being separated from the people who make us feel whole. One exercise Kabbalists recommend to help us feel Malkhut's position is to go some place to be alone. It's not just about getting away, but getting away with consciousness. Being alone not only gives us time to reflect, but it also give us appreciation for other people, because too much aloneness makes us hunger for company.

Malkhut is the sefira associated with the seventh day of Creation, Shabbat. Shabbat is the only day of the week mentioned in the Ten Commandments, so it must be important. But why? For six days God created the universe, but on the seventh day He created rest. It's an extremely significant idea that God created a day of rest. Think about it: on every other day of the week He created something huge—heavenly bodies, animal and plant life, human beings. But on the seventh day He simply created the concept of doing nothing. Why? Kabbalists say that in creating Shabbat, God created contemplation; He created a space for awareness in which we could take a step back from all that surrounds us and see His presence in it. The specific injunction in Orthodox Judaism is to not do anything on Shabbat that would alter your environment in any way or to not do anything that you would normally do on other days of the week, such as work or shopping or cleaning the house. There are many other injunctions for what should or should not be done on Shabbat, but in general they all relate to relinquishing our mastery over the world. In honoring this day of rest, we recognize God's handiwork in the world and His mastery over it. In doing so we enter a state of awareness and contemplation that can bring us closer to God. If practiced in the way it is intended, Shabbat can be an ultimate day of awareness; it is an entire day for practicing the Zen art of being in the moment and not being distracted by all of the other things that populate the rest of our week. It is said that the world is harmonized on Shabbat, and the channel between the physical and spiritual worlds is cleared on this day.

Because Malkhut represents awareness and the physical realm, one way we can experience Malkhut is to do an exercise in focusing our perceptions. You can do this either simply by focusing your awareness on each of your senses in turn, or you can do it more fully by taking a few minutes to do deep-breathing meditation and then focus your attention on your body. Take in all the data that is available to you. Take note of what your ears are hearing—the barking dog or the cars in the street, the footsteps in the apartment above. Then take note of the taste in your mouth. Are you still tasting the garlic from your pasta lunch or does the flavor belong to your mint toothpaste? Next, focus on your body sensations—the hardness of the chair or floor beneath you, the feel of your shirt on your arms. And what about your sense of smell? Is the air in your room stale, or is the window open? Is the air coming in through the window smoky from the chimney next door, or do you smell the dampness of freshly turned earth? Open your eyes and focus on the wall in front of you. Is the paint chipping or dirty? Is the wall textured or smooth? Kabbalah teaches that we should savor the sensual world around us and take pleasure in all that it offer us. To deprive ourselves of this pleasure is to invite repression and imbalance and to ultimately make ourselves closed off and ill. Sexual pleasure and good food and exercise and everything else that brings joy to the body and helps keep it fit without crossing into the realm of gluttony are all part of the holistic approach to maintaining a healthy balance. Indeed, sexuality is one of the strongest forces that courses through our universe and is viewed by Kabbalists as a fundamental aspect of who we are. Committed sex between partners is viewed as a healing act that brings about unification between the physical and spiritual, and helps bring individuals closer to God by focusing on their connection to each other.

CONCLUSION

Studying the various lessons that each sefira on the Tree teaches us can help us achieve balance in ourselves and help us recognize our connectedness to everything in the universe. As we work to become more aware of our bodies and emotions, feelings and thoughts, and of our place in the universe, we begin to recognize how our thoughts and actions not only harm or benefit us, but harm or benefit the world. The way we act toward one another has the ability to heal or hurt the divine. When I treat someone badly, I push Malkhut further from Tiferet, I cause the gap to grow wider and wider and I create further exile. The way to heal God, to make Him whole, is to first heal ourselves and our relations with other people. Healing is not just about becoming a more self-actualized person, it's about taking care of community. It's about giving and receiving.

When the world is unbalanced, the energy flow is impeded; when it's balanced, the energy flows evenly through all channels. We want the Tree to run like a well-oiled machine in which the energy comes down the center but touches on the left and the right as needed to balance itself.

The lessons that Kabbalah offers are not new; in the last few decades the world has recognized the same conclusions that the Kabbalists, and many others, arrived at centuries ago. What is so encouraging now, however, is that with the globalization of communication and information, and with our knowledge of what hasn't worked in the world in the past, we now have a situation in which we can really affect global change. But while we can keep this larger picture in perspective, we should never lose sight of our connection to the practice that needs to occur at home.

For some Kabbalists, the end goal in all of this learning and practice is to bring about ultimate unification. Ultimate unification, of course, refers to the Age of Redemption, the appearance of the Messiah, and a return to oneness. But for other Kabbalists, the practice of Kabbalah is simply a lifelong practice in which there is no final arrival. There is no race in Kabbalah. There's no timeclock and there's no finish line. There is only here and now, and every day brings new opportunity for growth and healing. The challenges of life never end, because life is dynamic. If changes ceased to occur, then the universe would cease to exist. As long as life continues, there is something else to experience and to learn. Today's task isn't tomorrow's task. Today the lesson may be one of humility, but tomorrow it may be one of boundaries and strength. We take the energy that comes to us, and we work to balance it. The realm of Keter and Ein Sof remind us that we can never reach a point when we know all there is to know; knowing all there is to know is not even an option for us in this realm. The task is simply to know what we need to know now to deal with the world that presents itself today, and then be prepared to deal with the different world that presents itself tomorrow. Don't look for the final outcome, these Kabbalists say, simply take care of your life as it is—direct your attention to your home and surroundings and community—and the rest will take care of itself.

In the end, we shouldn't forget that while all of this is an act of healing the divine, it is also an act of healing us and of healing the person to whom we give kindness. In Kabbalah it's all about grounding the teaching and bringing it back to reality. You do a little soaring to see the bigger picture, but then you come back to the ground to work on the smaller one. It's like a painter who steps back from his canvas to check his composition, to see that his colors are balanced, and that the picture is coming together as he intended. But once he does this, he then steps back to the canvas to continue working.

Everything that happens to us during the day has the potential for either healing or division. It's all about mindfulness and consciousness, to hold the separate realities in our mind, to be aware of the spiritual consequences of our actions, and be mindful of the bigger picture. When we see this, we understand that we are not helpless players but very powerful agents with the ability to alter the forces of the universe.

In the structure of this book, we began with the principles of Kabbalah on the higher levels, the cosmic levels, and are ending on the physical level. We have followed the Kabbalah injunction to keep things grounded. We've reached the end of the book, but at the same time have reached the starting point. The last chapter is really the first chapter, where the work of climbing the Tree begins. It is from here that we enter the gate of awareness.

The Talmud says that if we cannot articulate what we have learned, then we have not learned it correctly; if we cannot teach or give what we have received, then there is something missing in our grasp of it. If you can give it to other people, then you have fulfilled your role as receiver.

I hope that I've succeeded in imparting my understanding of Kabbalah in a way that enables you to see something of its beauty. While I don't expect this book to give you all the answers about Kabbalah, I hope it has given you the curiosity to begin looking for them in your own way.

NUMERICAL CHART
OF THE HEBREW ALPHABET

aleph	1		*samech*	60
bet	2		*ayin*	70
gimel	3		*peh*	80
dalet	4		*tzadi*	90
heh	5		*kuf*	100
vav	6		*resh*	200
zayin	7		*shin*	300
het	8		*tav*	400
tet	9		*end kaf*	500
yud	10		*end mem*	600
kaf	20		*end nun*	700
lamed	30		*end peh*	800
mem	40		*end tzadi*	900
nun	50			

GLOSSARY

Aleph The first letter of the Hebrew alphabet, which also represents the realm of infinity or of Ein Sof.

Assiyah The World of Manifestation; the fourth of the four worlds that Kabbalists say exist in the universe; refers to our physical world.

Atzilut The World of Emanation; the first of the four worlds, and the closest to God.

Baal Shem Tov Rabbi Israel ben Eliezer, the founder of modern Hassidism in the eighteenth century, who adapted many of Kabbalah's concepts to Orthodox Judaism.

Bet The first letter of the Book of Genesis and the second letter of the Hebrew alphabet.

Binah The third circle on the Tree of Life.

Briyah The World of Creation; the second world in the universe.

Drash The allegorical level of meaning of the Torah.

Ein Sof The Kabbalist name for God; means "without End" in Hebrew.

Ein Sof Or The light that emanated from God or Ein Sof in the process of creating the universe.

Elohim One of the ten names for God used in the Hebrew Bible.

Ezekiel A Jewish prophet who was exiled to Babylonia around 597 B.C.E. and who wrote about his encounter with God in the Book of Ezekiel.

Gematria A numerology method for obtaining deeper meaning of the Bible by substituting the letters of the alphabet for their numerical equivalent; numerical values are added and words with equal value are compared to discover deeper meanings in their relation to each other.

Gevurah "Strength"; fifth sefira on the Tree of Life.

Hebrew Bible The Old Testament, which includes the Books of Moses (the first five books of the Bible) as well as the books of the prophets and the psalms.

Heh The second and fourth letter of the sacred name of God, which propels the second and fourth levels of Creation.

Hesed "Lovingkindness"; fourth sefira on the Tree of Life.

Hochma "Wisdom"; second sefira on the Tree of Life.

Hod "Splendor"; eighth sefira on the Tree of Life.

Keter "Crown"; first sefira on the Tree of Life.

Malkhut "Majesty"; tenth sefira on the Tree of Life.

Merkavah mysticism A genre of mysticism, which emerged around the first century B.C.E. and continued to the tenth century, that sought to understand the nature of God and the heavens and the means to break through to the spiritual world.

Mishnah The oral interpretations passed on by Moses to the people at Sinai, which became the essence of Jewish law; written down around the second century C.E.

Netzach "Victory"; seventh sefira on the Tree of Life.

Pardes "Orchard" in Hebrew; refers to the realm of the divine as well as the different levels of meaning in the Torah.

Peshat The simple or literal level of meaning of the Torah.

Rabbi Akiva ben Yoseph A mystic who lived in Palestine from 40 to 135 C.E. and was head of the Sanhedrin council, the top Jewish legal council.

Rabbi Isaac Luria The scholar who refined and shaped Kabbalah in the sixteenth century; it is mainly his ideas and concepts that are taught today in a system known as Lurianic Kabbalah.

Rabbi Isaac the Blind The first modern Kabbalist, who lived in twelfth-century Provence, coined the word *Ein Sof,* and developed a theory of Creation as a process—from divine will to thought to the utterance of words—through which the world was created.

Rabbi Moshe Cordovero A Kabbalist who lived in Safed in the mid-1500s and who wrote a major compilation of Kabbalah and many original works of his own.

Rabbi Moshe de Leon Author of the Zohar.

Rabbi Shimon bar Yochai A second-century Jewish sage and protagonist of the Zohar.

Remez The metaphorical level of meaning of the Torah.

Safed A center for Kabbalah in northern Palestine in the sixteenth century; still survives today.

Sefer Ha Bahir (**"Book of Brilliance"**) A manuscript written between 1150 and 1200 that was a collection of mystical interpretations of the Bible; known as the first Kabbalist text.

Sefer Ha Zohar (**"Book of Splendor"**) The seminal work of Kabbalah, written around 1280 in Spain; covers topics such as the creation of human beings, the nature of good and evil, and the destiny of the soul.

Sefer Yetzirah ("Book of Creation") A short essay written between the third and sixth centuries C.E.; lays out a theory of Creation and the order of the universe. Much of Kabbalah's vocabulary comes from this work, including the naming of the sefirot, the elemental energy forces behind Creation.

Sefira/Sefirot The ten vessels through which the energy of God flows in the ongoing process of Creation, which are depicted as circles on the Tree of Life; from the Hebrew "to count."

Shabbetai Zvi A person of erratic behavior, born in Turkey in 1626, who claimed to be the Messiah and gained a large following of believers before being forced to convert to Islam by the Turkish authorities; his distortion of many of Kabbalah's concepts led to widespread mistrust of Kabbalah for many years thereafter.

Sod The secret or esoteric level of meaning of the Torah.

Talmud The book containing the Mishnah as well as legends, homilies, and commentaries on the Torah.

Teshuva Hebrew word meaning "repentance" and "return."

Thirty-two Paths of Wisdom The ten sefirot plus the twenty-two letters of the Hebrew alphabet.

Tiferet "Beauty"; sixth sefira on the Tree of Life.

Tikkun ha olam Hebrew phrase meaning "repair the world."

Torah Word meaning "law" or "teaching" in Hebrew; refers usually to the Books of Moses, the first five books of the Bible, but also can refer to all the writings of the Old Testament.

Tree of Knowledge The Tree in the Garden of Eden from which Adam and Eve were forbidden to eat.

Tree of Life The main symbol of Kabbalah; contains ten circles and twenty-two paths connecting them; depicts the forces of Creation.

Tzimtzum The "contraction" of Ein Sof, the first act of Creation, in which Ein Sof withdrew from Himself to create a finite space to begin Creation.

Vav The third Hebrew letter of God's name; propels the third level of Creation.

Yesod "Foundation"; ninth sefira on the Tree of Life.

YHWH The sacred four-letter name for God, which is composed of the past, present, and future tenses of the Hebrew verb "to be"; the name is vocalized as Elohim or Adonai; no one knows how to pronounce the name, though some people have translated it as "Yahweh" or "Jehovah."

Yud The first Hebrew letter of God's name; also the energy that propels the first level of Creation.

FOR FURTHER READING

The Essential Kabbalah: The Heart of Jewish Mysticism, by
    Daniel C. Matt. San Francisco: HarperCollins, 1995.
God Is a Verb: Kabbalah and the Practice of Mystical Judaism,
    by Rabbi David A. Cooper. New York: Putnam, 1997.
The Way of Splendor: Jewish Mysticism and Modern Psychol-
    ogy, by Edward Hoffman. Northvale, NJ: Jason Aronson,
    1989.
Zohar, The Book of Splendor: Basic Readings from the Kab-
    balah, selected and edited by Gershom Scholem. New
    York: Schocken Books, 1977.

ACKNOWLEDGMENTS

I would like to acknowledge and thank the following people for their help and support in writing this book:

Claudia Schaab, my friend and editor, who gave me the opportunity to share my long-standing interest in this subject. She helped shape the book, keep me on course, and made the process of writing it an enjoyable one.

Rabbi Eliahu Klein, one of my teachers, for sharing his enthusiasm for Kabbalah. Participating in the discussions in his class helped catalyze my approach to writing this book. My thanks also to Rabbi Klein for reviewing the manuscript and offering his comments.

Amit Morag, my home base in Israel and adopted sister, who has given me invaluable assistance throughout many writing projects.

Harold Glasser, my friend and employer, who generously gave me the time to work on this project and offered helpful feedback.

My brother Mark, who is a constant source of encouragement.

And finally, a heartfelt thanks to Guy Diament, who supported me in many ways throughout the writing of this book.

ABOUT THE AUTHOR

Kim Zetter is a journalist who has written extensively about issues related to Judaism and Israel for newspapers and magazines. Her interest in Kabbalah began more than ten years ago when she lived and worked in Israel among the Hassidic community. She currently lives in Oakland, California.

A Simple Wisdom Book

Simple Kabbalah is the third in Conari Press' Simple Wisdom Book series, which seeks to provide accessible books on enlightening topics.

Other titles in the Simple Wisdom Book series:

Simple Feng Shui by Damian Sharp

Simple Meditation & Relaxation by Joel and Michelle Levey

Simple Chinese Astrology by Damian Sharp

Simple Yoga by Cybèle Tomlinson

Simple Wicca by Michele Morgan

Simple Numerology by Damian Sharp

CONARI PRESS

368 Congress Street
Boston, MA 02210
800-423-7087   fax: 877-337-3309
e-mail: orders@redwheelweiser.com
www.redwheelweiser.com